# John Bunyan
## The Tinker of Bedford

## William Deal

Christian Liberty Press

Arlington Heights, Illinois

Printed by
*Christian Liberty Press*
502 West Euclid Avenue
Arlington Heights, Illinois 60004
www.christianlibertypress.com


ISBN 1-930367-59-7


Set in Garamond


Printed in the United States of America

# Contents

# Introduction

By any measure, John Bunyan was an unusual man. Having little formal education, he nevertheless wrote sixty books, one for each year of his life. Although he had no formal legal training, he helped secure a place for religious freedom in English law. Imprisoned for twelve years for refusing to obtain a "license" to preach, he nevertheless profoundly influenced his countrymen through the power of his pen, which no prison walls could still. Although he was ordained by no "officially" recognized denomination, he was among the most powerful preachers of his generation.

The son of a poor tinker, Bunyan accomplished more in one lifetime than most men could in ten. Yet whatever he did and wherever he went, conflict dogged his steps. Early in life he was sorely exercised about the state of his soul, but he could not shrug his burden of sin and was unable to find deliverance till he reached adulthood. In the English Civil War, he escaped death during a Royalist attack only because a friend had taken his place on guard duty—an event that powerfully brought home to him the meaning of Christ's atoning death. He was jailed repeatedly for preaching without a license. Though he was a skillful controversialist, engaging both Quakers and Anglicans, many of his writings were banned during his lifetime. Ugly rumors were spread about him by men who sought to undermine the effectiveness of his ministry.

Through these and many other trials, movingly recounted in these pages, John Bunyan remained faithful to his calling as he saw it. His dedication to Jesus Christ and fervor for the Gospel were acknowledged by even his most bitter enemies. And his vision endures in *Pilgrim's Progress*, one of the best-loved books in English.

The uncompromising courage and compassion of John Bunyan remains an enduring testimony to twenty-first century Christians who wish to impact the world for Christ.

The old rough cottage where John Bunyan was born disappeared more than one hundred seventy-five years ago.
(This image was taken from an old drawing.)

# chapter 1

Thomas Bunyan, the tinker, sat by the open fireside in his small home in Elstow, about two miles from Bedford, waiting for word from his wife. "How's Margaret now?" he called. He had laid down his tools some time before and expected at any moment the cry of a newborn baby.

"Very soon now!" the midwife called.

Thomas Bunyan was a large, muscular man—every inch a smith—with a shock of brown hair. He strode back and forth before the fireplace as Margaret, his beautiful young wife, cried with birth pangs in the room next door.

"At last!" shouted the midwife. "Come, Mr. Bunyan, behold your son." Thomas burst into the room and glanced at the wee thing with its astonishing shock of thick red hair.

"Ugh," he grunted, "Just like his Grandfather Bunyan—another redhead! Another hot temper to deal with!" Then turning to his wife, "A fine fellow, Margaret, what shall we call him?"

Margaret looked at her husband with large, luminous eyes. "I've been thinking about John. Do you like that?"

"John Bunyan," he said softly. "John Bunyan. An excellent name."

It was November 30, 1628. The Puritan Pilgrims had been in America eight years. There were religious uprisings in Ireland; the Presbyterians were battling for freedom in Scotland, and the English Puritans were facing rough times. Thomas Bunyan mused as he looked into the flickering firelight. "I wonder," he thought, "what kind of world will this wee one live to see."

Thoughts of the future blended with thoughts of the past. Elstow had originally been "Helenstow," named for St. Helena, the mother of Constantine. It was near the ancient Saxon church which had been dedicated to Helena long ago. Once a place of pride and station, it had gradually declined to its present insignificant state.

Bunyan's own small cottage was between two streams and at the edge of about nine acres of land. It had been in the family for centuries. Bunyan's ancestors had come from Europe about the time of William the Conqueror and had owned vast lands and a castle. All that was left of such fame and fortune now was a poor tinker and a small bit of land.

Bunyan's musings were interrupted by a loud knock at the door, which burst open to reveal a huge, redheaded man with a high forehead and deeply set blue eyes.

"Come in, Grandpa!" grinned Thomas, as the older Bunyan came into the room.

"How is Margaret? Any baby yet?" demanded Thomas's father as he pulled up a chair.

"A boy!" Thomas said, "A chip off the old block! Red hair like yours!" He led the older man to Margaret's side.

"Great day, if he's not another Bunyan from way back yonder," Grandpa roared.

"I was thinking how the Bunyan fortunes have wasted away," said Thomas. "From Norman knights to mere tinkers is a long step down, I'd say."

"Yes son, that's true, but then from 1066 to 1628 is a long time, and knights and lords can lose property and titles same as others."

"I could wish a better way of life for this poor babe," said Thomas, "but when one is low in England, there's no way to rise. He is sealed to his fate."

"True, son," said the older man rising to leave, "but no man's spirit need be sealed to a lowly life. Now I must go and tell Grandma the news. What's the name of the boy?"

"We've called him John, may it bring him luck," Thomas said with a wide smile.

"Huh, little luck can he expect in this world," was all old Bunyan replied. A few weeks later, little John was christened. Several remarked about his striking resemblance to his grandfather. Margaret Bunyan, conversing with the ladies about John, said, "He is already showing the spirit of his grandfather, very willful and determined. Thomas is so quiet and mild but Grandpa always liked to fight." Everyone laughed. Everyone in the village knew Grandfather Bunyan, and his quarrels and hot temper and loyalist views.

✠ ✠ ✠

Young John Bunyan grew up to the blaze of the smithy-fire, to the ring of the tinker's hammer and to many an itinerant jaunt through the countryside as his father traveled from place to place mending pots and pans.

Sundays found him in church. The sermons smelled of brimstone and fire. "You are a piece of iron," the rector roared one day. "You are heated white hot in the forge. You are being pounded flat. Hell will be worse than that."

"You are stuck fast in the slough," the preacher cried on another occasion. "You are caught in all the filth and stench."

Such sermons made a vivid impression on John. He was haunted by horrible dreams. "I dreamed I was in hell," he said to his mother. "The devil was there with a pitchfork. It was red-hot and he tried to stick it through me. I ran and ran. Jesus helped me out but I was scared to death." He thought a moment. "If I have to go to hell I think I'd like to be a devil rather than one of his victims."

John's father thought the boy had better stop listening to the stern old preacher. "No, Thomas," said his wife. "We just need to teach him repentance. The boy already has a hot temper and is quick to pick up bad words from the older boys."

✠  ✠  ✠

One day, the door opened and in stepped Grandpa and Grandma Bunyan, who had come home late. When they visited it was always a time of great fun for the children. While Grandpa Bunyan was quarrelsome and a man of bad temper, he was a kind and interesting storyteller for the children.

"Well, well, what brings you two over at such an hour?" Thomas Bunyan asked. "We were just preparing to send the children to bed, but now this will all have to be changed. They would never sleep a wink if they did not hear a good-night story from you, Grandpa," Thomas said as he offered them chairs before the large open fireplace.

Young John's grandparents had seen a hanging in Bedford. "You know the Suttons?" said Grandpa. "Well, the old man heard the rector preach in St. Paul's on the judgment of God. He came under conviction of sin and confessed the horrible crimes he and his wife had been committing for years. Remember the burning of the Johnson home? Robbery and murder were involved in that. Sutton confessed to the crime."

"Why that was five years ago," Margaret cut in, "just after little Margaret was born."

"Yes! and they did it." Grandpa said. "The rector told old Sutton to confess to the authorities. They hanged both of them today. It was horrible."

"When I reached the village green I saw a large crowd," Grandpa continued. "There was a scaffold and two people were standing near it. I watched the sheriff place a black hood over their heads. One of them was a woman. The man standing beside me said it was her request that she be hanged with her husband, for they were equally guilty."

"Were they old people, Grandpa?" John asked, eagerly listening to every word of his grandfather's story.

"Oh, I'd say they were not too old, maybe fifty years," Grandpa replied. "But the thing that was so hard about it was what happened when they got them both up on the scaffold. They made a double scaffold so they could hang them at the same time. Just as they placed the rope around the woman's neck, she started screaming. 'O God, I'm lost, I'm lost, I'm lost—I am soon going to hell! Oh, why have I lived such a life?' Then the sheriff's deputy placed the rope about her neck and stepped off the scaffold. The man said nothing. Then they pulled the trap door from under their feet and they both hanged. Ah, I never want to see such a sight again. The awful words of that woman burn in my ears. 'I'm lost—I'm lost. I am soon going to hell!' I cannot get these words out of my mind," Grandpa said as he sat gazing steadily into the open fire, as if he were looking toward something far beyond the fire in the fireplace.

Margaret quietly handed the large family Bible to Grandma. The devotions were from Galatians, "For whatsoever a man soweth, that shall he also reap."

After prayers, Margaret said, "All right, children, come now, get to bed. Tomorrow will be a happier day. Maybe Grandpa can find us a better story if he comes tomorrow night."

John asked one parting question before leaving the room. "Grandpa, what will happen to these people? Will they go to hell and be burned forever?"

"I don't know, son. All I know is what the woman said just before she died," Grandpa explained. "I hope God granted her repentance. I saw her bow her head and mumble something just before the deputy put the rope around her neck."

John had a bad night. In his sleep, he relived the story of the hanging. Several times he thought he heard the woman screaming, "I'm lost—I am soon going to hell!" Near morning, he dreamed that the devil came

4

to his bed and was about to take him away to torment. "You have been swearing and telling lies," the devil said to him. "I have come for you. I will torment you forever!" John awoke screaming so loud that his mother was awakened.

"Oh, Mother," he sobbed, "the devil has just been here to get me and I jumped clear of him. He was here for real, Mother. I saw him and heard him," he cried. "He was red all over and had horns and a long fork in his hands. I saw him right here by my bedside. When I jumped up, he left, Mother. Please pray for me. I have been very mean."

"What have you been doing, my boy?" she asked, sitting down beside him in the dark room, on his bedside.

"Oh, Mother, I have been telling lies and swearing, and other bad things. I feel I will be lost in hell, like that poor woman Grandpa saw hanged yesterday."

"If you have been doing these things, John," his mother said quietly, "you must ask God to forgive you, and then you must stop them. These are sinful things and you must not do them."

"But Mother, God will not forgive one who has been so mean. I am a most sorry and no good boy; I cannot stop these things. I hear them in my head and I want to do them in my heart. Oh, Mother," John lamented, "am I already too bad to be saved?"

"No, of course not. Jesus said He would forgive all manner of sins. Now you trust in Him, and He will give you peace in your heart." She sat by him on the bedside and prayed with him.

The effect of the dream wore off as John went about the day's activities. He was a little sad, but his mother said no more to him of the dreams.

# chapter 2

The years slipped by and soon John was ten. Often during these years the growing boy was haunted by frightful dreams in which he saw dark scenes, devils with horns and pitchforks and cats that turned into demons.

One night Thomas Bunyan said to Margaret, "John's ten. It's about time the lad was sent to school to learn his letters."

His opinion was strengthened the next day when young John demanded, "What's a king supposed to do?" He had heard his parents discussing King Charles's problems with the Dissenters.

"See there, Margaret?" Thomas said. "He doesn't even know what a king is. I tell you we must send him to school. We're sending him to the grammar school at Bedford."

"But Master Vierney is so hard on children, he beats them," Margaret said. "I've already taught John to make his letters. And he can read some."

Thomas arched his eyebrows.

"But I think you've another reason for sending him there," Margaret continued. "Master Vierney is a King's man, a loyalist, and you want John to be a strong King's man, too."

Thomas grinned. His wife could read him like a book.

Shortly after this, John found himself walking to Grammar School at Bedford. John's friend Tad had gone to school there for two years and had learned a lot.

"John, ye best not tell Master Vierney that you be not a King's man," Tad warned John. "Master Vierney is a loyalist and he expects all his scholars to be King's men, too. If they are not, he beats them till they at least *say* they be King's men." Young John's independent spirit had already imbibed some of the liberal views of the Dissenters. Tad knew this and sought to caution his friend.

The school building was a small stone house with three small windows on each side and a door in the front end. It had two windows in the back. All the windows were high enough that one could not see out of them when seated at the desk. John and Tad joined other youths pouring into the school.

Master Vierney rose from his chair when all the students were seated. John looked him over. He was tall, raw boned and had a large, reddish nose. His deep-set blue eyes shined out from beneath shaggy eyebrows and sandy hair. He had large, ugly hands. John wondered just how hard he could hit a fellow with his stick.

Just then Master Vierney bellowed out, "Get your slates and line up at the table." John lifted his new slate from his lap and rose with the other boys.

"I see we have a new scholar today," Master Vierney said as he looked toward John. "Tell us your name, son," he demanded.

"I'm John Bunyan, Thomas Bunyan's boy. He's the village tinker at Elstow," John replied.

"I know, I know," Master Vierney roared at him. "I did not ask for your family history, boy, just your name. If I want more information I will ask for it," he said. "And you say, 'sir' to me, or I'll pull your ears till they ache," he scowled.

He came toward John, brandishing his stick. "There is one thing every boy in the grammar school must learn, young fellow," he said. His cold blue eyes fastened upon John. "In this school every student is to be a King's man, and never anything else. Are you a King's man?"

"Ye know that my father be's a King's man, and I'm loyal to my King," John said.

"Not *ye* know, like a country hooligan, but *you* know; and not *be's* loyal, but *is* loyal," the school master shouted at John.

"Yes, sir."

"Now, I want to know, are you just loyal to the King, or do you believe the King has absolute right to rule all men, even without a Parliament?" Vierney asked, frowning.

"What's a *Parleyment?*" John asked.

"*What?*" shouted the schoolmaster, raising his stick as if to strike John. "Do you mean that you are so ignorant you don't even know what Parliament is? *Parli-ment*—not Parleyment—is the group of Lords and Commoners who are elected by the people to advise the King on matters of rule when he asks for it," Vierney explained.

"Doesn't the King need these men to advise him? Even a king cannot know everything, can he?" John asked quite frankly.

"The King rules by divine right from God. He knows what's best for the people. He only needs Parliament to help enforce his laws," Vierney answered.

"I asked are you a King's man? Do you believe in his absolute rule?" the master thundered.

John cringed. He knew that to argue was to invite the stick on his back, so he meekly said, "Yes, I believe he has absolute right to rule the people."

"That's better!" Master Vierney said, lowering his stick. "We are all loyal men around here. We will allow no traitors in this school." He brandished his stick and glowered at the class. Young John Bunyan got the message. The schoolmaster was an intolerant bigot and a bully who would use his stick to enforce his views.

✠ ✠ ✠

John continued to have bad dreams. "Last night I saw the flying buttresses of the Abby chapel with great big eyes in them, looking at me as if I had committed all the sins of the whole world. All of a sudden, the very earth broke apart and I began to sink down into a great chasm, into hell, I guess it was. Then, a bright and shining One flew from a white cloud in the heavens and reached down and got hold of me and drew me back out of the great hole. He said to me, 'Come unto me and I will give you rest.' Is that in the Bible, Mother?" John asked, looking longingly at her.

"Why, yes, son, this is found in Matthew 11:28. It is Christ's promise to the sinner. All you have to do is to repent and believe on Him, and you can be saved," she explained.

"I'm going to stop swearing," John promised.

But in a few days John had forgotten the dream and even his promise not to swear, and was at it as loud as ever with the village boys.

✠ ✠ ✠

All went well in school for several days. John had mastered his alphabet completely and was quickly learning to read and write better. He was becoming the best reader in his grade.

One day the matter of religion came up. Tad asked Master Vierney why he was opposed to the return of Parliament to power. "If the Parliament helps the King to rule well, then why do you not want Parliament to be recalled?"

"We do not need a Parliament, our King is a sensible man and he can rule us far better than any bickering, money-wasting and quarrelsome Parliament," Vierney shot back at him.

"My mother believes in Parliament," John said quietly.

"She has no right to believe in this since her husband is a King's man," Master Vierney said. "She should be subject to her husband and believe as he does."

"Why can't a person think for himself, even if there is a king? The king cannot think for all the people, can he?" John asked.

Master Vierney's face turned red, his anger growing all the while. "Young fellow, it is treachery to speak like this of our King. Of course he can think for all the people in matters that concern us politically. We will not allow such talk here, do you understand?"

"My mother is not a King's man, even if Papa is, and while I am loyal to my King, I think people have the right to think for themselves," John blurted out.

"So you are a fence straddler, are you?" snarled the schoolmaster. "We have no place in England for fence straddlers. You'd better decide for the King, boy, or your neck may stretch from a rope."

Vierney looked around and fastened his eyes on Tim Sutton, whose father was known to be a Puritan. "You there, Sutton, does your father have a right to work against the King by demanding the recall of Parliament?" the teacher asked.

"He has the right to use his own mind and do what he thinks is best, doesn't he, sir?" Tim said cautiously.

"The King is the head of the Church of England. Your father has no right to go to conventicles† and refuse to attend the proper church," Vierney snapped.

"My father has to obey his conscience in such matters. The King is not his God," Tim said quietly.

There was a considerable pause. The boys were horrified to hear one of their own defy a King's man like Master Vierney with such bold words. They shuffled in their seats and several coughed.

"So he can disobey the King and act as he pleases, and still he is a worshipper of God. You think that, do you?" Master Vierney shouted at him, coming closer and gripping his big stick.

Tim was fourteen years old but he was poor and not too strong. His deep blue eyes were quiet and kind. He looked the teacher in the eye.

† A *conventicle* is a religious worship service that is held in secret without the authorization of the state church, in this case, the Church of England.

9

"That's treason, the same kind of bunk the traitorous Scots say," yelled Vierney, his face red with rage. "I'll have no such talk in this school!" He grabbed Tim by the hand and yanked him off his wooden bench.

In cold rage, the master thrashed the young offender into unconsciousness. Melvin Crowley, one of the bigger boys, had had enough. Leaving his seat, he caught the bullying schoolmaster a blow that felled him to the floor.

That was the end of Vierney's reign of terror. The school board replaced him with a Mr. Jones who, although just as cruel, was able to keep his temper on a better level—not that it made much difference to John. His school days were almost done, for he was old enough to join his father in the tinker trade.

✠ ✠ ✠

The small Bunyan land holdings which belonged to John's father were at a site commonly known as Bunyan's End. It was in the east end of Elstow Parish, not far from Harrowden, where once flourished the Saxon church, dedicated to St. Mary and St. Helena, until around the time of Henry VIII. Queen Mary had given this land to Sir Humphery Radcliff, whose widow lived there until about the end of the sixteenth century. Her son sold the property to Sir Thomas Hillersdon, who had a fine stone mansion built on the property.

John loved to fish in its ponds, despite the fact that Sir Hillersdon had forbidden all such trespassing. Forbidden or not, on this October morning as the sun rose brightly over the eastern hills, John decided he would try for some fish in Sir Hillersdon's pond.

Suddenly the young poacher's peace was disturbed. He sprang up in alarm, an alarm tinged with awe and admiration as he recognized the intruder.

"Never mind me, my lad," the stranger said. "Let's see you catch a fish. What's your name, boy? How do you pass your time?"

John said, "I'm the son of Thomas Bunyan the tinker. I help him in his work." He waxed confident. "I guess I'm a bad boy, sir, trespassing like this. I'm afraid I swear and steal apples, too."

"That's wrong, son," the stranger replied, "but then boys will be boys. I hope you'll grow up to be a fisher of men."

That day, after getting a thorough soaking in the pond, John caught a fine fish. He recounted his adventures to his mother. "You'll never guess

who fished with me today!" he cried. "No, I expect not," his mother replied.

"None other than Oliver Cromwell himself," John replied excitedly.

"*Cromwell?*" Margaret exclaimed. "Was he nice to you?"

"I reckon he was. See how wet I am? I slid into the pond and would have been drowned if he had not been there to pull me out," John explained. "And he got this big fish I was wrestling with when I slipped into the pond."

✠ ✠ ✠

About a month after the above incident, word reached Bedford and Elstow that the Earl of Strafford had been imprisoned for treason. Secretary of State Windebank had gone to France; Archbishop Laud was locked up in the Tower; and Finch, the Lord Keeper of the King, had fled to the Continent. Things were moving fast now toward a showdown with the King. Parliament passed a law that no bishop could sit in the House of Lords. Another law was passed providing that no subject could be taxed without the tax being levied by Parliament. Parliament also passed an act whereby it would never again have to wait for the King to call it into session. Even some in the King's own army were plotting against him. By mid-spring, Strafford had been executed by the King's consent, though he was a "King's man." Confusion reigned. Some of the men of Elstow shouted, "Strafford is dead, he will do us no more harm!" Others mourned his death, among whom were Thomas Bunyan—he too was a King's man.

London was in an uproar. Almost anything could happen. Civil war was almost certain now. The House of Commons swore to protect political liberty and the freedom of religion. The King still believed in the divine right of the kings and toyed with the idea of war to prove his point.

About that time John made the annual summer boat trip with his father to Lynn to buy metal for use in their work. John listened to the conversations of the men on the boat. At Great Bradford another tinker boarded the vessel and had hardly been aboard when he said, "Thomas, have you heard there is likely to be war between the King and Parliament?"

"Surely Parliament would never risk that," Thomas Bunyan said, lifting his shaggy eyebrows.

"Ah, you never know," a farmer cut into the conversation. "The Queen has just left for Dover, taking the crown jewels to trade for munitions, so I heard."

"The two Houses of Parliament are now united in their stand against the King," another passenger said. "How can we avert a civil war?"

"The Cavaliers have deserted the King, and the King told Parliament that, if he granted all their wishes, he'd be no more than a phantom king," the man from Great Bradford said.

"Why can't the King and Parliament get together; what is the use of a civil war? It will settle nothing," another passenger said.

Thomas Bunyan thought best to keep his thoughts of his King to himself for the rest of the trip.

During the last part of June, the Bedfordshire men in the House of Commons appealed to the people in what they called the Grand Remonstrance. Its purpose was to give the King a chance to save face by relieving him of all the blame for the common grievances of the people and placing the blame upon his advisors and counselors.

But the King did not listen to the pleas of the common people. That August, at Nottingham, he raised his standard and the Civil War began.

✠ ✠ ✠

The September heat brought weakness to Grandpa Bunyan. He complained of pains in his chest. During August he had helped Thomas now and then in his work. He went to the Ouse River with John twice to watch its waters course under the famous old bridge at Bedford. The jailhouse sat on that bridge, a jailhouse which also served as the tollhouse where tolls were taken from riverboats, many of which carried grain to London. But now Grandpa kept to his house.

November brought bright clear weather. John's birthday would soon be coming and Grandpa walked to Bedford to look for a gift for John.

About midnight that night Thomas Bunyan was awakened by his mother beating on the door of his home. "Come quickly, Thomas, something has happened to Grandpa!" she shouted. The whole family rushed to Grandpa's house. Grandpa's eyes were glassy and his head was cold and very damp. Margaret laid her hand upon his brow and shook her head. John came up to the bed just as Grandpa gave a small sigh and his breath left him.

"He's gone," Margaret said, as she walked away from the bedside.

John broke into tears. "He can't be gone—not Grandpa!" he cried as he laid his hand on Grandpa's face. It was cold and clammy, and John knew his Grandpa was dead.

Grandma was weeping softly as she approached John. "Here, John, I'm going to give you this now. Grandpa walked to Bedford and back today to get this for your birthday." She handed him a beautiful book which Grandpa had bought for his birthday, *The Seven Champions of Christendom*.

John grasped the book in his hand and walked to the fireside where he could look at it for a moment. Then he wailed out in his boyish way, "My last gift from Grandpa!" A moment later, as he sat by the fireside, John prayed silently, "O God, help me to be like Grandpa!"

The night his grandfather was buried, John dreamed that he saw him riding a large white horse and carrying a trumpet in his hand. He was

13

dressed in a long, flowing white robe and was so happy and smiling as he glided by where John was standing in the churchyard. "May there be peace on earth for all men," he heard his Grandpa shout as his horse rose and disappeared into the blue heavens.

Meanwhile, England was girding for war. By January 1643, the battle lines were being drawn between King and Parliament. Men of stern will and strong conviction opposed each other, and the temper of the people was rising.

One day in springtime, John Okey rode into Elstow and stopped his horse by Thomas Bunyan's house and forge. Thomas Bunyan looked at him sourly and said, "*Now* what do you want, swords for Roundhead soldiers?"

"All of Bedfordshire is for Parliament," said Okey. "We have gibbets† ready for those who aid the King."

Bunyan contemplated his anvil and the low burning fire of coal in the forge. Looking up at Okey he replied, "I guess I was being somewhat hasty."

"Parliament needs the support of all good men," Okey replied.

"I can't make swords to fight my King," Bunyan said stubbornly.

"Very well, Bunyan, I will give your word to Cromwell, Pym, and Pampden. I have delivered my message," Okey said as he mounted his horse.

John had stood by silently and heard it all.

"But why be for the King, Papa, when you know he is not for the common man and the poor, such as we are?" John asked.

Thomas Bunyan drew a deep breath. "Get this straight, lad," he said. "For generations the Bunyans have stood for their King."

"Yes, sir, but Grandpa felt that Parliament was often right and that the King was often wrong, didn't he?" John ventured.

"Your grandpa did sometimes feel this way, but he never lifted a finger against his King," Thomas Bunyan chided.

John said no more, but his mind was made up. "When I am old enough to fight I certainly will not fight for the King," he mumbled to himself.

✝ ✝ ✝

---

† A *gibbet* was a type of gallows consisting of a single post with a projecting arm at the top; it was formerly used to hang executed criminals in chains for public display.

The spring of 1643 brought smallpox to the Midlands. John was frightened. Times were uncertain. Cromwell, his idol, was now a captain in the Parliamentary Army. Captain Cromwell's son was stationed at Newport Pagnell. John was stunned one day when word reached Elstow that Cromwell's son had died of smallpox.

"Will we get smallpox and die, Mama?" John asked that evening as he came in from work, when the news had been brought about Cromwell's son.

"I hope not, son. But if this is the way the Lord wants to take us, we should have no fear," she said. This was of little comfort to John. He did not want to die of smallpox; he wanted to die for a noble cause, like helping Cromwell win the war. He knew better, though, than to voice such an idea in his father's presence.

A few days after this, John met his old friend Tad Simmons, now a Roundhead soldier.

"Cromwell is a colonel," announced Tad. "He's got fighting stuff in him, John. He'll lead Parliament to victory for sure. He is asking for godly men to join his army. Each soldier gets a Pocket Testament and a small Catechism and is supposed to attend church regularly."

"Then what are *you* doing in his army, pray tell?" John asked, grinning up at Tad. "You're a rascal. You cheat, lie, steal and drink, and even run around with women."

"That doesn't matter, John. A fellow can still handle a gun; good gunmen are needed, as well as praying men," Tad laughed.

✠ ✠ ✠

During the fall of 1643, the Royalist army made an attack on Bedford, mostly to secure food. Prince Rupert, the King's nephew, was in charge. John happened to be on the road between Elstow and Bedford one afternoon when he saw a group of soldiers coming toward him. They were dressed in the King's Army uniforms. John thought they were beautiful.

The soldiers stopped, and one of them asked John if he knew where the Bedfordshire food was stored.

"I don't know, sir," John replied.

"Do you speak truth?" the soldier asked.

"I don't always, but I do so now, sir," John said, his heart pounding so loudly he wondered if the soldier could hear it.

Just then a soldier in blue rode up on horseback. His boots were shiny and his high hat looked immaculate. The soldier who had been speaking to John addressed the newcomer as "Your highness, Prince Rupert." John's heart leaped. "Prince Rupert! Now I'll have a story for the family at suppertime. I have seen Prince Rupert face to face," he thought as the Royal Cavaliers rode away. After this John was more interested than ever in joining the army.

✠  ✠  ✠

The spring of 1644 found John Bunyan working six or seven hours a day with his father in the forge, mending kettles and pans and doing other work and wishing for November when he could be a soldier. In the evenings he read whatever came to hand or played with Margaret and Willie, the youngest Bunyans. He often read to them from his birthday book, *The Seven Champions of Christendom.*

One day Tad Simmons came by for a chat. He was stationed at Newport Pagnell, at the Parliamentary Army Post. "Oliver Cromwell talks about God as if he knew Him personally," he said. "And Sir Samuel Luke—you know him—he's confident we'll win this war. He says God told him we'll win."

John told his mother about Tad's visit after supper that evening while his father was still at the forge. He noticed she was warming a brick by the fire. "What's the brick for, Mama?" he asked.

"It's to warm my feet, John. I am so cold all over," she replied.

The next day she was worse. After supper she lay down again and asked Margaret to place the hot brick to her feet. Margaret felt her face. It was flushed with temperature.

"What shall we do, John, Papa's gone to the alehouse and you know what that likely means—midnight before he returns," Margaret said. "She has no spots on her but what if she has the plague?"

John felt his stomach tighten. "Where would she get that?" he whispered.

"It's everywhere," Margaret explained.

"I'm going for Dr. Banister right now," John said.

The doctor examined the large, red, boil-like lump on her leg. "The *plague*, sure enough," he muttered to himself.

Just then Thomas Bunyan staggered in at the door, drunk.

Margaret went to him and said, "Papa, Mama has the plague." Her father looked at her with bleary eyes and sank into a chair by the fireside.

John came out of the bedroom and stared unbelievingly at his father. "Papa, Mama may be dying now of the plague, and here you are drunk!" he exclaimed.

Some time later, Thomas Bunyan emerged from his drunken stupor and sat bolt upright in his chair. "Where's Margaret?" he asked. The doctor came forward and said, "Your wife has the plague. It's time you pulled yourself together and tried to be of some comfort to her."

Staggering into the room, Thomas fell across Margaret's bed and wept like a child. "Forgive me, oh, forgive me, Maggie dear!" he cried. "I did not know you were so sick!"

Lifting her feeble hand, she laid it on his face. With great effort she said, "I'm going now, Thomas, I'm going ... going to Heaven.... Meet me there...." Her voice trailed off into a whisper, and soon after she was gone.

"It's all over, children; your mother is safe on the heavenly shore," the doctor said quietly.

Thomas Bunyan staggered from the room wailing, "Oh God, I can't stand it, I can't stand it!"

Two days later, Margaret Bunyan was buried. That night sobs shook young John's frame, and he shivered in the cool night air. His sister Margaret heard him crying and came to him. Placing her arms around him she said, "O John, please do not weep so hard. We shall see Mama again. It will not be long."

"But I am so sinful, I shall never see her again," John sobbed.

"But John, 'the blood of Jesus Christ, God's Son, cleanseth us from all sin,' it says in the Bible. It will cleanse you, too, and you will see Mama again some day," she said, comforting him.

That night John dreamed that he saw the angels escorting his mother to her mansion. She looked back toward earth and said to them, "Don't forget my son, John. Bring him, too."

The angel said, "He is on the list. We will help him come."

When John awoke he felt great joy for a moment, but then he remembered it was only a dream—a dream which may never come true.

# chapter 3

A low fog hung over the sea. John Bunyan and Tad Simmons had galloped from Elstow to the ocean on Tad's horse. Tad had Saturday off from army duty and they intended to make the most of the day at the seashore.

"Ah, man, how I'd like to cross that ocean and land in the brave New World," Tad said as he tied his horse to a tree near the beach.

"Not me. I guess I'm too scared of water, ever since I almost drowned that time when Cromwell pulled me out of Hillersdon's pond," John reminisced, as they undressed and put on swimming suits that Tad had stolen from fellows in the army.

John could not swim, so he was dependent on Tad to watch out for him. They waded out until they were shoulder deep in the water. They rode a couple of waves, bobbing up and down to keep their heads above water.

Then Tad saw a rugged wave coming, towering far above their heads. "Here it comes, John, hold on for all your might." John grabbed Tad's hand and was holding firmly as they rode the crest of the wave. Just then John gulped a mouthful of sea water and began to choke. In his excitement, he let go of Tad's hand and the undertow dragged him on out toward the sea. His head bobbed up in the water and Tad saw that he was far out beyond the shallows. "There he is away out there, guard," Tad shouted.

It was touch and go for a minute, but they finally dragged the drowning lad to shore. He was almost unconscious, his lungs had taken in water and he was breathing only short breaths and with great difficulty. The guard began to work with him, holding his head downward so that the water would drain out of his lungs. After several minutes, John became composed once again.

A man came by with a flask of ale. "Here, fellow, take a good draught of this; it will help you." John drank deeply from the flask and then lay down on the sand again. He was very weak and nervous. Soon the ale brought color to his face again and he sat up.

"I almost didn't make it, did I Tad?" He rubbed his eyes and looked around.

"No, you didn't, John."

"I know I'm wicked and a contemptible wretch, Tad, but I reckon God had some reason for sparing my life. I can't see what for, God knows I see no future for myself. Maybe I'll go into the army and die for my country," John said weakly.

✠ ✠ ✠

During the remaining summer days John and Margaret often spoke of their mother. "You know, John, I find myself almost continually thinking of dear Mother. It was hard to lose her, but she's so much better off where she is. Papa seems to be forgetting her awfully fast. I saw him talking with Anne in church this morning. He seemed very happy just to be near her. I wonder what will happen to torment us next."

John sometimes took Willie fishing in Cardington Brook, bringing home a string of fish for Margaret to fix for supper. One morning when they came home with a good catch, Margaret looked wanly at John and said, "Clean it, John, I'm just too tired to do anything." John looked at her in astonishment. She went and lay down on the bed.

Later John went in to see her and took one look at her face. It was red and hot. "You've got the *plague*!" he cried.

"Oh, John, surely not," Margaret managed a smile.

John rushed across the field for Dr. Banister. After examining her the doctor confirmed John's diagnosis. "It's the plague all right, and I fear a bad case of it," the doctor said.

Papa was deeply disturbed. "How can God take away my wife and now, perhaps my daughter, in so short a time, when we need them so much?" he grumbled. "Look after her, John," he said as he walked out of the door to go to the forge.

"John, you had best go away, so you will not catch the plague," Margaret said. "You must live, even if I have to die. I don't mind dying, for then I can go to be with Mother in heaven." Margaret was more mature than her fourteen years often betrayed.

"Never mind me," John said. "I'm strong and healthy. I can stand it and besides, I'll not get the plague." He slept but little the next few nights as he kept watch over her.

19

Dr. Banister came in early one morning. The huge boil-like lump on Margaret's leg had burst. "Get boiling water, John, and prepare some rags to clean Margaret's leg. It's a good omen when one of these nasty things breaks."

"God," John prayed, "let my Margaret live. I'll stop swearing, and lying and stealing."

In spite of all John could do, his sister died. He dropped to his knees by her side and began to swear bitterly. He was about to say, "God, I hate you," when little Willie spoke up and said, "God does all things right. He needed Margaret for an angel, so He took her, John. Don't you understand anything?"

John got up from his knees. Looking down at Margaret's peaceful face, he placed his hand on her forehead and said, "Good-bye Margie ... *forever!*" Then he turned and went out of the room.

Great sobs shook his body. "Oh, God, I can't stand it. You took Mama, now You take my Margie; take me and be done with it!" he cried as he walked out the back door. Papa stood speechless and silent, great tears rolling down his face.

Several mornings after, the three Bunyans sat at the breakfast table. "We sure need a woman around here," Papa said. "Pretty tough sledding for us fellows with no woman in the house."

"But Papa, I'm doing my best to learn to cook, and I'll soon be doing better," John said. Willie said nothing but looked at John.

One evening soon afterwards, when Willie had gone to bed, John sat reading his book, *The Seven Champions of Christendom*, by candlelight, when the door suddenly opened and Papa walked in followed by a large woman about his own age. "Still up, John?" his father greeted him. "This is Anne—you remember her—she's your new mama. We were married this evening."

"How are you, Johnny boy?" Anne said, smiling at him. John remembered her from the times he had passed the alehouse. He had nothing against her. Maybe she was a good woman, but he couldn't see how Papa could have married her so soon. Mama had been dead scarcely three months.

"Aren't you going to speak to me, John?" the woman chided.

"Oh, yes, hello. I was in deep thought, and I was so surprised, too, that Papa would marry so soon," John said awkwardly.

"Yes, I know how you feel, John. But your father needed a wife. I'll be good to you and help take your mama's place. You won't have to cook

20

and do dishes and keep the house any more. That ought to make you glad," she said, patting John on the shoulder.

"Well, that's that," John thought, going upstairs. "Papa has his wife and she can care for Willie. Now I am free to join the army as soon as I'm sixteen—and I wish that were tomorrow."

A few days later, John was walking in the woods near their home when he was bitten by an adder. His father tied the leg tight above the wound and ran for help. Thanks to the doctor's skill and Anne's tender nursing, the youth recovered. Soon he was able to walk again. "You have been a good nurse, Mama Anne," John heard himself telling Anne one day, almost in disbelief at his words to her.

"Oh, thank you, John dear. It makes me so happy for you to call me Mama," Anne said as she patted him on the shoulder. "I guess you just remind me so much of my real mama," John said, half embarrassed.

After this John was much more contented with his father's selection of Anne for a wife.

✛ ✛ ✛

At last November came and John was sixteen—old enough to enlist. He knew there were recruits soon to leave Bedford for Newport Pagnell, so in mid-November he slipped off one afternoon to the recruiting station in Bedford. Despite his father's Royalist leanings, young John had long since decided that Cromwell was the man for him.

"I want to join the army, sir," he said to the recruiting officer at the station.

"Very well. Answer these questions." The officer drew out his quill. John listed his name and parents and his home residence. "Your age, young man?" the officer asked. John swallowed hard. "I'm sixteen," he said. The officer did not quibble about it for John was a large boy for his age. "And are you a pious boy?" the officer said. "Cromwell wants pious young men in his army," the officer said sternly.

"Yes, sir." John lied again. "I attend church regularly, read my Bible and pray always, sir."

"Then you can read?" the officer asked. He handed him two little books, *The Soldier's Pocket Bible*, and *The Soldier's Catechism*. "Make sure you read these well, young man," the officer said. "Now go and get your medical."

The army doctor's examination was a routine thing and over in a few minutes. John was issued a pass card bearing his number and regiment. "Report at nine o'clock tomorrow. We leave at ten," the doctor enjoined.

That night, John's old dreams returned to torment him. He dreamed that he was in battle. Men were dropping dead all around. Finally, a musket bullet hit him and he keeled over dead. In a moment, he was sinking downward into the flames of hell. He saw Christ standing over against the other side of the heavens, but his face was turned from him. John cried and begged for forgiveness, but Christ paid no attention. Then he thought of his wickedness and that he had sealed his doom. Soon the devil appeared, laughing with fiendish glee. "Ah, you are mine now, and you're not getting away this time. I shall burn you in the deepest hell forever," the devil laughed.

When John awoke, great beads of perspiration stood on his brow. He lay for a long time thinking of this horrible dream. First, he thought he would mend his ways and try prayer and Bible reading, but then he thought it would be of no use, for most of his army friends would not be Christians, and why should he make a mock of religion, when his heart was as wicked as the devil's. So he decided to put off the matter of religion till he finished his army service at least. With this decision, there seemed to come a peace of mind, and back to sleep he went. It was almost daybreak when John awoke again. He rose in haste, scribbled a note to Anne, asking her to take good care of Willie, and saying he hoped she and Papa would be happy. He told her he was going into the army, and not to worry about him. Leaving the note on the kitchen table, he then slipped out of the house with his small bundle of clothing and was soon lost in the low hanging mist of the November morn.

At ten o'clock the men started marching for Newport Pagnell.

About halfway there, a soldier taunted him, and John's anger flashed. He swore at him.

The Captain wheeled on his heel and looked at John sternly. "There will be no swearing. This is God's Army. Young man, two shillings fine from your first pay for this! You'll learn your lesson. And furthermore, hear this: There'll be no drinking, stealing or lying, and no molestation of women and girls."

John's hot temper flared. Almost automatically he bellowed out, "Aye, Captain, I'll obey your orders in battle and in camp, but no man shall tell me what to do or think beyond this, not even the King nor Cromwell. I know Cromwell; he will not forbid a man to think for himself!"

The Captain glared at him. "Your name, young man!" he bellowed.

"John Bunyan, sir, son of the tinker of Elstow," John snapped back.

"Men obey orders in this army, Bunyan," the captain growled. "You'll not only lose two shillings from your pay, but you'll ride the wooden horse. Make a note of that, Sergeant."

John walked on in silence, almost wishing he were back home with his father.

A short while later, John rode the wooden horse. This was a large contraption, consisting of two rough boards nailed to four wooden legs. John was placed upon this frame without benefit of a saddle. A large placard was hung about his neck, proclaiming in bold red letters BLAS-PHEMER. A musket was tied to each of John's feet, pulling his weight downward, and his hands were tied behind his back. The Captain then read his sentence and the soldiers shouted, "Aye, Aye, so let it be to this blasphemer!"

"Upon the third offense the victim's tongue shall be cleft," the Captain roared as he strode away. The Drill Sergeant then released John and got him down from the wooden horse.

Tad was lingering behind to greet his old friend when John got down from the wooden horse. "Well, a right good introduction to army life at that, John. Come, now, and I'll take ye to mess hall. Then, tonight we can find some girls and have us some fun till curfew time."

"Yes, Tad, I'll go with you to get acquainted with the army service centers but not the girls. I never did this in my life. Wicked though I am, I'm not going to start that."

Left to himself that night, John felt a wave of homesickness. He perused the pious platitudes of *The Soldier's Catechism*. He was supposed to memorize it but had no wish to do so. He glanced at *The Soldier's Bible* and found it full of moral and pious advice. He thought for a moment about starting each day with prayer, about crying to God for help in battle, about Jehovah as a "man-of-war." Then he put the book away as well. So this was Cromwell's army.

Several evenings a week, John spent till almost curfew time in a nearby book shop reading. He was one of the few who did this. Most of the soldiers could not read.

✠ ✠ ✠

John dreaded the long haranguing chapel services each Thursday night and Sunday. Every soldier was expected to go, if he had sufficient clothes. If he could find a good enough excuse, though, John preferred to remain in the barracks. Sometimes, he secured leave to attend the regular services of St. John's Church in the city. Here he met other young people and found himself by no means unpopular, for he often proved himself the life of the group.

One Sunday at St. John's, he saw two girls come in. They sat behind him, and he was annoyed by one of them talking during the service. Once he turned and glanced at them, and the girls became quiet. Afterwards John walked out of the church and was met at the end of the pew by the two girls. They looked to be about fourteen or fifteen years old. One of them was tall, with dark brown hair and soft brown eyes. She had been much more quiet during the service than the other one. Her eyes caught John's as they met at the end of the pew, and he stopped for a moment to allow them to precede him out of the church. They were shy and did not precede John as he had expected. They stood for a few seconds staring at each other.

Finally, a smile lit up John's face and he extended his hand to the tall girl. "I'm John Bunyan, a soldier stationed at Newport Pagnell garrison."

"My name is Mary. I live with this girl, Arlene," the tall girl said as she gave her hand. John held the graceful, slender hand in his for a long moment.

Releasing his hold on her hand, he asked, "Is this your home, or are you a visitor here?"

"You might say its my home now. Arlene is my cousin. My father died recently and left me alone, so I came to live with my relatives here. My mother died of the plague a year ago. I am alone now, except for my relatives," she explained.

John swallowed hard. A lump came into his throat and his eyes moistened. "My mother and sister died of the plague last summer, too," he said. "Do you work here, then?"

"Oh, I work here in a store. My father sent me to a girl's school until last fall when he died."

"Then you must be older than I guessed you," John said. "I thought you were fourteen or fifteen."

"No, I am past seventeen now," she said, with a smile. Her teeth were even and she had a beautiful complexion.

"Do you girls attend church here?"

"Every Sunday generally," Mary answered. "We have been away and have just come back."

John glanced up at the church tower. "I must run or I'll miss the noon meal. I'll see you here again some Sunday soon, then, if all goes well," John said as he waved good-bye.

The next Sunday, John was early for church. He looked everywhere but did not see Mary and Arlene. Perhaps they were only fooling him. He put his mind to the service and was not aware when the girls came in. When the vicar finally said "Amen," John glanced around. His eyes met Mary's and held for a long moment.

When the service concluded, someone spoke to John and he was held up a moment. He was regretting every moment of the time, and when he had politely withdrawn from the man speaking to him, he hastened to the door. The girls were standing on the large steps. John walked over to them and said, "Here you are. I almost missed you."

"We saw you, but we didn't mind waiting for a moment, or at least I didn't," Mary said, smiling at John. "Arlene wants to go home soon, but I'm not in any hurry today. It's so beautiful outside for a winter day," she concluded.

"Oh, I'm glad you are not in a hurry. I have the day off," John said, his heart speeding up.

"Were you thinking of something?" Mary said. John was not aware of the faraway look in his eyes.

"Oh, it's nothing. I was just thinking of a crazy dream I had," John laughed.

"A dreamer, eh?" Mary teased. "I've heard dreamers are the best actors and writers. Are you a writer?"

"Me, a writer?" John laughed. "I've never written anything! I never thought of it seriously, but now that you mention it, I believe I could write if I had anything of interest to write about."

"I surely think you could, John. There you go, dreaming again," Mary teased him. He was unaware that he had been silent.

After a moment he said, "Mary, you are almost an exact picture of my sweet sister, Margaret, who died last summer. I miss her so much. I guess you somehow sort of take her place."

Mary dropped her head for a moment. Tears came into her eyes. Then, looking up into John's face, she said, "I'm glad I mean something to someone, John. I often feel so unwanted. Forgive me for crying like a baby."

"Mary, you have done nothing for which you need my forgiveness. You have given me something more precious than gold," John said.

"What's that?" she asked, smiling at him.

"Assurance, that I, too, mean something to someone. My father married again within three months of my mother's death. I felt unwanted, too."

"Then, we can thank God for each other," Mary said.

John took Mary's hand in his and held it firmly for a moment. "I understand, Mary. We are friends, and I hope we always shall be," he said, allowing her hand to slip out of his.

"How far is it to your home, Mary?" John asked, fishing for an invitation to walk home with her.

"Only about a mile," Mary replied. "Arlene, could we invite John for dinner today? Do you think your mother would care if we did?" Mary inquired.

"Of course we can!" Arlene assured Mary. "There's always plenty and Mother loves company."

"But your father is a King's man and a Royalist supporter. What will he say if we bring a Roundhead soldier for dinner?" Mary bantered. They all laughed heartily.

Arlene solved the problem, saying, "John has no uniform; we'll not tell Father that he's a soldier."

As they walked home they discussed war, peace, and the common questions of the times.

"My father was a King's man, and I guess I inherited some of his ideas," Mary laughed broadly. "But I suppose the Parliament men have some good ideas, too, and maybe they are partly right, who knows?"

"My father too is a King's man," John explained. "But there aren't many King's men in Bedfordshire. My grandpa was a Parliament man and I guess I have his leanings."

"Oh, well, we'll not allow this to break up a good friendship," Mary laughed.

"You are really a pretty good philosopher, Mary," John laughed.

✠ ✠ ✠

On Monday of that week, there occurred a flareup of activity between the Royalists and the Parliamentary soldiers. All Parliamentary soldiers were restricted to their base. John did not see Mary for over three weeks. A Christmas truce was signed by both sides December twentieth, and all soldiers were given liberty.

John came into town and went directly to Morrison's store and bookshop where Mary worked. Mary kept the bookshop. When he saw she had a spare moment he went to her to explain that he had been detained at the base. "You don't need to make any explanations, John. A skirmish took place right here in town and some soldiers were killed in front of this store. So I knew you were kept to your base. I just prayed that you'd be safe."

"Mary, I've been thinking an awful lot about you while I've been on guard duty and shut up in the garrison," John said, moving a bit closer to her.

"Well, then, we are even, I guess. I've been thinking a lot about you, too."

"I am happy that you'd think of me at all, even after you found out that last Sunday we had together what a knave I really am," John said, dropping his head, for he had confided in Mary that he had been a swearer, thief, liar and a ringleader in all such bad things in his village. Mary had said softly to him, "John, it hurts very much for you to tell me this, for I have come to admire you a lot. But look, John, anyone who is able to be a ringleader for doing bad is also capable of doing great good and becoming a leader among men for the good way of life."

Though he took some comfort from these words, he almost regretted his confession. "Have you been thinking, Mary, that you must send me on my way, since I'm not a King's man and such a bad fellow?" He waited for what seemed an eternity while Mary attended to a customer.

Finally she came back. "Now, Mr. Bunyan, I can answer you properly. It's almost closing time and we'll have no more customers, but I don't have to go home for an hour yet so now we can talk in peace."

John waited apprehensively, wondering what she would say. His heart was pounding wildly.

"I've just missed seeing you at church and missed talking with you. I've been praying for you each night and every morning. I still believe, John, that some day you will become a leader among men," Mary said.

John was grateful she had not said she could not see him again. But was this her way of ending their relationship? He always seemed to look on the dark side of life.

"Are you dreaming again?" Mary smiled. He heard her soft voice as though from a distance.

"I guess so, Mary, pondering whether or not you are going to send me away."

"Of course I'm not going to send you away, not now or ever. I want you—I *need* you—for a friend, always!" Mary said, laying her hand upon his arm.

"Thank you, and God be thanked, too," John said, taking Mary's hand into his and holding it tightly. For a long time they stood quietly talking.

"I guess we had better go now, John," said Mary at last.

"Maybe I'll see you again tomorrow," John said as they parted at the door. He felt as if he were walking on air as he hurried back to camp.

The next day was December twenty-third. John found Mary not busy for a moment. He pulled out of his pocket a neatly wrapped package and gave it to her. "This is my Christmas gift," he said, "I'm going home for Christmas and will not be back until about January first. You know there's a truce till January seventh. I wish so much I could take you to see my home and my folks, but there is no way I can now—maybe later."

"I'd love to meet them," she replied. "There's plenty of time for that."

On Christmas morning Mary waited till Arlene left the room to open her gift from John. She could scarcely believe what she saw—a pure silk head scarf, from India, one of the finest imports. She rubbed her skin with its dainty softness. "God bless my dear John," she prayed softly. "And to think I didn't even give him a single thing!" she murmured to herself. She remembered the light in his eyes when she told him she would never send him away from her. Then she knew she had given John something better than any material gift she could have afforded— the assurance that she did care for him. Had Mary only known then how hard John was working to win her confidence, her heart would have throbbed a little faster. But this was a secret John was keeping in his heart, locked up between him and his Lord.

✚ ✚ ✚

Early in February John was in town one day and saw Mary for a few minutes in Morrison's store. "Know what, John? Next Friday is my birthday. I'll be eighteen. Arlene and her mother are having a special party for me, and we want you to come." Mary's brown eyes danced.

"Mary, that would be so wonderful," John said, "but I'm on guard duty all this month. If I'm not on duty that day you can be sure I'll be there."

"Oh, I do hope you can come. Can't you exchange with someone for a night?" Mary asked.

John left in high spirits, thinking about how he could work it out.

He had a good friend at camp named Fredrick Sheppard, of Worcester. They spent many happy evenings together, reading or discussing things of interest. Moreover, Fred was a godly young man who wanted to win John to Christ, and John did not oppose his approaches, for Fred always seemed to know how to talk to him—especially when he was moody and needed help. As it happened, John's name was on the Friday

28

duty roster and, sure enough, Fred did take his place. John was grateful for his unselfish friend.

"I can't thank you enough, Fred. But are you sure you should have done this?" He sat for a long time thinking of how kind Fred had been and of how he must repay him in some way. Possibly the best way to repay him would be to become a real Christian at heart, he thought.

The stars were beginning to come out as John neared the Bradford home. It was a large two-story grey stone house. It had been there for many years. The Bradfords were an old family in England. John recalled that he had heard his father refer to Jonah B. Bradford of Newport.

Mary was wearing a beautiful new dress which her aunt had given her. John had never seen her more beautiful. Her dark brown hair fell to her shoulders; her brown eyes sparkled with delight, and she looked taller than he had ever seen her in the long, slender dress. She cast a glance in John's direction with a big, winsome smile. He knew this meant for him to be content and she would see him later. Just now she must not make a scene of their friendship. As the evening progressed, Mary managed to get near John a couple of times. Each time, she touched his hand and whispered to him some little thing which made his heart leap for joy.

After the refreshments had been served the gifts were brought out. John almost sank through his chair as he saw the lovely gifts opened. Arlene was in charge of presenting the gifts and had saved John's till last. As she opened it, Mary's eyes grew large. Arlene pulled out of the wrappings a beautiful silver cup. Then she slowly drew out the name and read aloud: "To the most wonderful girl in the world. From John Bunyan." Mary's eyes sparkled with delight. "Oh, it is so *beautiful!*" she exclaimed. "Thank you so very much, John. How did you know that I have always wanted a cup like this?" John was so overcome with embarrassment that he could not say a word.

The evening went quickly. Soon it was nearly nine and John had to leave. He did so much want a few words with Mary before he had to go. The crowd began milling around in the large drawing room. Mary came over to John, seized his hand in hers and gave it a hard squeeze. "Oh, John, you have made me *very* happy tonight. I'm sorry I couldn't come to you sooner, but you understand, don't you?"

Giving Mary's hand a long, warm squeeze in turn, John said, "I must run now, if I'm to get back to the barracks on time. Oh, I should tell you how I was able to come. My friend, Fredrick Sheppard, from near Worcester, is standing guard for me tonight."

"Fredrick Sheppard? I know him. He lived not far from us once. He's a fine Christian. You must thank him for me, too."

John reached the barracks just before the guard locked the gate. He slipped in and went to bed without lighting a candle. Pulling the covers up over his head, he soon fell into deep slumber that lasted till morning.

During the night the Royalist guards made a skirmish raid some distance from the barracks. Some Royalist soldiers were killed—and one Parliamentary guard, Fredrick Sheppard.

John broke into sobs when he heard the news. "How can it be, how can it be?" he cried. "He died for me; he was on duty in my place! Had it not been for him, I'd have been a corpse myself this very morning."

"Possibly true, John," said Captain Miles, the garrison commander, "And have you stopped to think that there was another, Jesus Christ, who once took your place? He, too, died for you, John. He was your Savior."

"Yes, I know. Fred often talked to me about Him. I've wanted to serve Him, too, but I am so wicked at heart," John sobbed out his sorrow. "I'm trying to break off sinning, and I mean to serve Him," John said. Miles lifted his hand from John's shoulder.

"See that you do, John, and I shall remember to pray for you," Miles said, as John left the office. "God must have some work for you to do, the way He spared you."

✠ ✠ ✠

Two weeks later, on Friday afternoon, John came into the store at Morrison's. As soon as Mary was free he went to her. She had already heard the account of Sheppard's death and knew by now most of the details. John began to weep as he came near Mary. She placed her hand on his shoulder. "Please, John, try not to take this so hard. God has His ways, and we do not always understand them. Fredrick is with the Lord, and you are spared," she said.

John lifted his head and looked into Mary's brown eyes. "You remind me of my mother, Mary. She was like that, with simple faith in God. Oh, if only I had that faith!"

"It will come, John, it will come. Keep on praying for it."

"Mary, you sound more like a Puritan than an Anglican," John said.

"There are Puritans in the Anglican Church, John, and doubtless, there are some who are Anglicans among the Puritans. Does that help any?"

"I guess that's the best explanation I've heard yet," he said.

"Don't forget, John, I am praying for you each day," Mary said as John started to walk away.

"Thank you, Mary. It helps so much to have someone who understands in a time like this. I just felt I *had* to see you again. I'll see you in a few days if all goes well."

"Try not to worry, John. Trust in the Lord, remember?"

In the weeks that followed there was almost no activity between the armies. For a while John's sleep was troubled by vivid, horrifying dreams. Soon these passed away but left him melancholy. As spring approached, John often walked in the fields near the garrison when off guard duty. There he prayed, meditated, and sometimes read from his *Soldier's Pocket Bible*, which he carried constantly. He sometimes read from the *Catechism*, too, but mostly from the *Pocket Bible*. He stopped swearing, lying and stealing. He also stayed away from the Village Green, for dancing was a temptation to him.

᛫I᛫ ᛫I᛫ ᛫I᛫

The fortunes of war took John and his companions to the north of England, where the Roundheads engaged the King's Royalists in heavy fighting. Many men were lost; but, at last, Cromwell—now a General—soundly defeated the Royalists. Hundreds lay dead on the field of battle. John's heart ached with deep sorrow for the wounded and dying. He had escaped injury except for a few scratches.

In the fall, the soldiers returned to Newport Pagnell. John missed Tad Simmons, who had been left on the field of battle, wounded. He wondered if he had survived or not. He missed Mary, too, for he had not seen her since late spring.

As he walked into town, the second day after his return, he saw Mary coming down the walk toward Morrison's store. She had not seen him, so he darted in between two buildings until she came even with him. He dashed out, saying, "Halt, Little Miss, and give an account of yourself!"

She fairly jumped at him, grabbing his arm and shouting, "How dare you scare a lady, you Roundhead soldier!"

"Oh, I'm so glad to see you again, Mary. I've often thought of you since I've been away."

"Well, at least its good to know I've not been forgotten, John. I've thought of you, too, each day," Mary said.

John slipped his arm around Mary and they walked slowly toward the store two or three blocks away. They talked of many things.

31

That evening, John took Mary to the Lion's Head where they had dinner. Mary was working until nine o'clock that night, and John had a special midnight leave. After store hours, John and Mary walked home. The moon was bright, and they walked arm in arm down the country road. John told Mary of his struggles to live a good life and of his occasional relapses into sin. But he assured her that none of these had been serious and he had tried to repent and pray after each such time. Mary was content to believe him, replying that to repent after sinning was all anyone, however saintly, could do.

At the gate where he left her for the night, John took Mary into his arms. He had feared she would resist him, but to his surprise she did not. He started to kiss her but she turned her head. "Not on the lips, John," she whispered softly. He then kissed her cheek and she patted his cheek in return. "God love you and keep you," she said.

✛ ✛ ✛

The winter months passed with little activity. Spring found John and Mary often walking home after Sunday services at St. John's. With the coming of summer, the garrison at Newport Pagnell had been ordered to Ireland. But just as suddenly, and without explanation, it was ordered demobilized and its men dismissed from the services. John was mustered out of the army in July 1647, with a month's advance pay. He was now nearly nineteen and felt a sense of aimlessness. He was not sure what course to take. He knew no trade but that of a tinker, and that not very well. But there was no other course open to him than to return to Elstow and hope his father would help him get a start. Possibly he could then get a business of his own in time.

His dismissal from the army had come in the middle of the week, but all the soldiers had been told that they could remain over the weekend. It was Thursday evening before John finally saw Mary again. She was just leaving Morrison's when he caught up with her, saying, "Not so fast. Where are you going?"

"John, how you do like to pull tricks on me!" Mary cried.

"And why not? I like the good-natured way you take them."

"I've been thinking of you this afternoon quite a bit, John."

"I hope those thoughts were not too bad."

"I never think anything but good thoughts of you, Johnny. You know that."

"Well, just what have you been thinking? You know I've been dismissed from the army and that I'll not be around these parts much longer. We are allowed to remain in the barracks over the weekend, then I guess I'll go home to Elstow," John explained.

"That is just what my thoughts were all about. I'm wondering when I'll ever see you again after you leave here," Mary said, her large brown eyes fixed on John.

"We will be together, Mary, but not as often as before. I have no horse and no way to travel but on foot, and twelve miles is a long way to walk."

John spent Sunday with Mary. They walked in the woods and sat on a log by the pond. John held her hand in his a long time as they sat silently by the pond. At last Mary asked, "Are you troubled, John?"

"I guess I am," he answered. "I was just thinking of how much I'll miss you when I go home tomorrow. I'll have no one to go to when I'm so despondent. You have always cheered me up. I love you very much, Mary, but that is all I can say now."

"I love you, too, very, very, much!" She squeezed his hand. He put his arm around her and they sat quietly for a long time. Then he kissed her tenderly on the cheek.

"It's so hard to see you go. Newport will be so lonely for me with you gone, John."

"And how do you think Elstow will be for me without your smiling eyes and dimpled cheeks to greet me? You will be very much in my thoughts, day and night."

They rose from the log and walked to the house. John said good-bye to Mary at the gate. Then she ran into the house. He sighed heavily. "If I could only support her, life would be more tolerable," he thought to himself as he trudged on toward the garrison.

The next morning, John bade farewell to his comrades in arms and set out for Elstow on the noon coach.

# chapter 4

W ord had already reached Elstow that the Newport Pagnell garrison had been closed before John arrived home. The Bunyans had expected John in on the Saturday stage, but he had not shown up.

"Wonder what's keeping John so long at Newport?" Thomas Bunyan said to Anne as they sat down to breakfast on Monday morning.

"Could be he's found work to his liking there, or maybe some friend is holding him up, like as not," Anne said as she poured the coffee. "If I know John, he'll be here before long," she said as she passed the steaming hot coffee to her husband.

"Willie, did you look in on little Thomas Junior as you came downstairs? Was he still sleeping?" Anne asked Willie, who had just made his appearance at the table. Willie was twelve now and was in school in the winters but helped his father part of the time during the summer. Elstow now had a small school for the primary grades.

After breakfast, Thomas went to his forge and Anne to the housework as usual. At noon a group of children and a few adults gathered at the village store for the arrival of the stage from Newport. As the carriage arrived, several people stepped off. Willie, who had come to see if John might be on the stage, was disappointed and had started to go when the last passenger stepped off the stage. He was a well-dressed soldier of the Parliamentary Army, boots shining and hat setting high on his head. His new uniform looked fresh and the matching shirt made it even more attractive. Willie turned to glance once more at the shock of reddish-brown hair sticking out from beneath the hat. Running toward him, he cried, "John, I almost didn't know you in that—that—what's ye call it."

"Oh, my uniform, you mean?" John answered, going over and patting Willie on the head. "You've really grown up, too, boy, in the past four years."

Everyone welcomed John with open arms, when finally, uniform and all, he came marching home. He picked up Thomas, Jr. from his cradle.

"Good addition, I'd say," said John, rocking the baby in his arms. All the old bitterness about his father's early remarriage had long since gone. He knew Anne had made his father a good wife. Willie had completely accepted her as a true mother, though he still called her Mama Anne.

Papa came in from the forge just as John arrived and greeted him warmly and with a touch of that deference men pay to sons who have grown up away from home.

"Pull up a chair, son. Put your feet back under the old home board. Don't expect ye got too much good food while ye was in the army, did ye?" He looked with pride at his grown-up son and said, "Well, I never dreamed I'd have a son that would fight against the King."

"I'm a Parliament man, Papa, just like Grandpa was. I believe in the rights of the people and the individual's freedom to do as he wishes," John said testily.

"Well, I'm a King's man. I guess I'll die one. I think this is the best system for the people. What do most people know about how to use freedom, as you call it, if they had it?" Papa wanted to know.

"It's not a matter of how they use it; it's that they must have it, to be a free nation, Papa, you know that."

"Thomas, ye best not argue with him. You know his mother taught him to think for himself," Anne said as she felt the tension rising.

"Well, I guess ye are right, Anne. He's too grown up for me to teach him anything. And besides, he can read and I can't, and that makes a deal of difference, I dare say."

"Did you see any girl to suit your fancy down there in Newport, John?" Anne asked.

"Ah, yes, there's one girl there that I really like. She's past eighteen and beautiful. She has long dark hair, and brown eyes and is tall and graceful."

"Did ye find out about her parents?" Papa wanted to know.

"She has no parents, Papa. Her mother died in the plague and her father was killed over four years ago. She lives with the Jonah Bradfords at Newport. They are her aunt and uncle," John explained.

"No dowry, then," Papa said.

"No, but I didn't ask her to marry me, Papa, so let's not get too fast with it. She is deeply religious, and that is something not every girl can boast of being. She finished two years of school, too."

"Yes, I'd say that's so," Anne put in. "Girls hardly ever go to school, unless they are from wealthy homes."

"Will you marry her, John, and bring her here to live with us?" Willie wanted to know.

"I don't even have work," John grinned.

"You are welcome to work with me, John. I'll make arrangements for ye to get a share of the pay for yourself."

"Thank you, Papa. I'll be happy to work with you. I want a day or so to visit some old friends first, and then I shall be ready to buckle down to work."

"Very well, son, I'll be ready for ye when ye are."

✠ ✠ ✠

John began work the last of the week and remained a steady worker for some time, but he had moody spells and his father could not understand him. When he was in his moods he would pull into his shell and say, "Don't try to talk to me. It's no good. I want to be left to my thoughts."

John increased his swearing and drinking. He did not often get drunk, but he drank ale almost daily. He even returned to his pranks of boyhood and was once discovered actually ringing the old church bell. It had been quite a while since Mary had written him. He was getting restless, and his mind was in turmoil.

In August, John received a reply from Mary, to a letter he had written her. The letter filled John's heart with excitement for it was long delayed. She had sprained her arm, she explained. He had thought Mary's failure to reply meant she had forgotten him and their courtship was over. It had hurt him deeply. Now, he had new life. He would go to Newport and see her.

John had worked hard and now owned most of his tinker's tools. But he needed an anvil, so he went into Bedford to get one. After he made his purchase, he headed for home. While walking along High Street, however, he decided to stop in at the local bookshop.

The shopkeeper's wife was a vile woman, of low character, who carried on with peddlers and hangers-on at inns and with immoral men. Moreover, John found some of her children playing within the shop.

As he was looking at the books, the anvil slipped and fell, striking his toe. John exploded in a string of vile oaths.

"Ye wicked wretch!" the woman shouted at him. "The Devil take your obscenity. Get away from our shop. Your profanity spoils all the youths of our town!"

John hung his head and limped on down the street, his cheeks burning with shame. Here was an immoral woman rebuking him for swearing.

A few days later he said to Anne, "Since that wretched woman rebuked me for swearing the other day in Bedford, I find I'm leaving off swearing to my own great wonder. Possibly God will yet work a work of grace in me."

"Of course He will, John, if ye only believe in Him to do so," Anne said comfortingly.

✠ ✠ ✠

Early in September, John caught the stage for Newport Pagnell. Despite his ale-drinking sprees, John had managed to save quite a bit of money. He wanted to set up a shop of his own. All the way to Newport, he kept thinking what he would say to Mary when he saw her again.

The stage arrived mid-morning and John walked the mile to her home. He found Mary getting over a cold.

After the noon meal, they went for a walk. "Oh, Mary, I was so distressed when I did not hear from you," John said. He took her hand as they crossed the road and headed for the pond and the wooded area beyond. "I feared you had decided that such a no-good scoundrel as I was not worthy of your care, and that you had thought best to break off with me, and not writing was your way of telling me. I know how very unworthy I am and how pure and good you are."

"Stop it, John, right now! I am no better than you are. Only by the blood of Christ has He saved me and made me His own. John, why don't you believe in Christ and be saved now?"

"I try to be good, Mary. But I like my ale bottle and my sinful companions too well, I guess. I go to church every Sunday and I do want to be saved, but it's so hard when you have no one to help you."

She took his hands in hers and held them tightly. "John, dear, don't you know Christ loves you far more than I do or ever can? If I am willing to accept you because I believe in you, will Christ not do likewise?"

They stood for a long moment, saying nothing. Then John turned to her and said, "Mary, please give me one more chance. I promise I will try harder this time. But oh, you don't know how dreadfully hard it is to break the habit of swearing. When I lose my temper it just seems to come out all on its own."

"I am praying for you every day, John, and I shall never cease. It is my prayer that the Holy Spirit would help you understand that salvation comes by faith in the atoning work of Christ. He died in your place; it is His work that saves you, not you striving to establish a righteousness of your own, based on good works."

Her words seemed to burn in his heart, as he longed to have the same faith as his beloved Mary. She reminded John so much of his mother that his thoughts carried him back to the times when she would comfort him with words of Christ's mercy and forgiveness. "All you have to do is to repent and believe on him," she would say, "and you can be saved."

As they strolled on by the edge of the woods, John abruptly changed the subject. He began to tell Mary of his work with his father and of the tools he had been able to purchase. "I plan to open my own shop as soon as I can become sufficiently established and get all the needed tools. I must have many more, and they are not easy to get. I have been saving most of my money."

"That is wonderful, John. You are doing fine and I admire you so much. Old Mr. Morrison always says you have the makings of a wonderful man some day. He knows how you love books, and one day he told me he thought you might even become a writer."

"I'd love to write, Mary, if I were educated. I often wish I had stayed in school longer. I've forgotten so much of what I learned. Occasionally I do find myself writing out my thoughts on various subjects, but then I throw it all away. It seems so useless. But I do like to try it now and then."

"That is wonderful! Please save some of your writings for me. I studied the great English writers in school and learned how they came to write. Many did not think they could write when they were young, but they kept at it and finally became famous authors."

"Sometimes I can write verse, especially when I'm thinking of you," John said.

They were now seated on the huge log beside the pond. Mary was humming an old English tune. John sat in silence, listening to the melody of her voice. His mind drifted away in a happy reverie.

"John, you're daydreaming again," Mary gently chided. She laughed into his ear.

"Oh, I was just remembering a little episode in boyhood when I was fishing one day in the Hillersdon pond. A farmer was there fishing with me. I caught a large fish and while trying to wind it in, I slipped into the pond. If he hadn't been there, I guess I'd have drowned."

"And who was your rescuer?" Mary asked.

"None other than the great General Cromwell himself. He used to live over near us and often fished in the pond."

"Cromwell! Really? It was he who fished you out and saved you? No wonder you are a Parliamentary man, John! Maybe I would be a bit more sympathetic if someone like Cromwell had saved my life, too."

"No, that is not really the reason, Mary. I was a Parliament man before then. My grandpa was one, too, and he taught me many things about freedom and the rights of the common people."

"But the King allows people their rights. Doesn't he allow his mother to have her Catholic services and her priests, even though he is an Anglican?" asked Mary.

"Let's not get into any political arguments, Mary. Our time is too short."

"All right, as you say, John. I think there are many fine people who are for Parliament. Did you know that you told me this story once before, John? But I love to hear you tell it anyway. I guess it makes me feel that you are very important when you tell it," Mary laughed.

Next day, John went with Mary to church. He met several old friends from the army. Finally, Mary was able to pull him away, reminding him that they would be late for dinner and this would make her aunt unhappy.

That afternoon, after the girls finished the dishes, John and Mary strolled over to the old log. John was in better spirits. He had laughed and been very merry most of the way home and after dinner. While they walked toward the log John said to Mary, "You know, there's a little thatched house in Elstow near our home that I'd like to own some day. It's just across from the big slough there and in plain view of the woodlands beyond."

"Why don't you buy it, John?"

"Buy it? Darling, I haven't the first pound to place down on it, much less to buy it. I guess I was merely dreaming again." John laughed a hearty laugh.

A robin sang merrily in a nearby tree. The sun was warm in the afternoon sky. John reached for Mary's hand.

"Mary, darling, I have been thinking for a long, long time about something. My mind is fully made up now, so I must speak to you about it this afternoon." The robin flew to another tree and started his song again.

"And what is so important as to engage your mind like that, I wonder?"

"You, Mary, you! I need you so very much to help me in life, if I am ever to be happy or amount to anything. And yet, how can I ask you to share my miserable existence with me? But, I'd rather be dead than not to have you." He lifted her hand and kissed her fingertips lightly for a moment. Mary sat very still, waiting for him to go on.

After an interminable time, Mary said, "Do I really mean that much to you, John, dearest?"

"Yes, darling, you really do, and far more, but no words will come to say it. All I can say, dearest love, is that I want you for my wife more than I have ever wanted anything in my life. Do you believe you could possibly share my life with me? Can you trust me that much, Mary, dear?" His deep blue eyes were looking steadily into hers. She saw his eyes moisten with tears. Great tears welled up in her own eyes, too. Her head found its resting place on John's shoulder.

Lifting her face to his a moment later, she said, "You have paid me the compliment of a lifetime. I have been out with a number of boys, but from the first day we met, I knew you were different. I have always liked you very much. That liking has grown into a deep love. I could never be happy apart from you. Yes, John, dear, I will be your wife."

John took her into his arms. His lips found hers and they sealed their love with a deep kiss of devotion. For a long time they sat motionless, her head resting upon his shoulder. The robin sang out cheerfully. Mary lifted her head and said, "Well, Mr. Robin, you sing as if you were enjoying the good news." John laughed a deep, satisfied laugh and pulled Mary close to his side.

"Well, dear, we must begin making plans for the wedding. Since I'm going to marry you and I need you now, I'll plan to come for you in about three weeks. How much time do you need?" asked John. "Are three weeks enough?"

"It will not take me that much time to get ready, John. You know I have no dowry to arrange. I have not so much as a teaspoon, nor a knife nor fork."

"Then why don't I come for you in two weeks? Can you arrange for the wedding by then?"

"Yes, John, I can wear my party dress Auntie gave me and we can get the vicar of St. John's to perform the ceremony, for I must be married in the Anglican faith, John, do you mind?"

"Mind? Of course not. I was brought up all my life in the Anglican Church."

"And John, there's something else, too. I shall always be for the King, you know. But women have no vote, so I guess that part doesn't matter."

"Certainly not, Mary. You know that I am a strong believer that everyone should have and hold his own opinions about such things. What do you think I fought on the side of the Parliament for if not for this right?"

The next day John caught the morning stage to Elstow, arriving at noon. At the supper meal John told his father and Anne about his proposal to Mary and their plans for marriage. Then he went to the owner of the little thatched house and asked to rent it. The owner consented and John began immediately to fix it up. Before the two weeks were up, he had a bed, and almost everything else which they would need. He was cheerful as he helped his father in the forge by day and worked on the little cottage in the evenings until dark. He made a small writing table for the attic and a candle holder. John was never so happy as during those two weeks of preparing to bring his bride home.

On the Friday before the wedding, John borrowed his father's horse and wagon and set out for Newport Pagnell, arriving there at sundown.

He went straight to the home of Mary's auntie, where a gay party was to be held for Mary that night. Several of her friends brought in small gifts, and the evening was a most pleasant one.

The next day, at ten o'clock, the family and a few friends gathered in St. John's Church, where the vicar performed the simple marriage ceremony. After dinner, John and Mary started for Elstow, arriving there well before sundown. John had kept the news about the cottage a secret from his bride.

On the way home, Mary worried about what they would do. John merely said, "Where is your faith, Mary? Don't worry, we will make it fine. We can even live with my parents for awhile." He grinned to himself.

They were met at the Bunyan home by a host of friends. Anne had set them a wedding supper and many friends welcomed Mary into the community. Afterwards, John took Mary to their new home, carrying her across the threshold and setting her down in the midst of the living room. Mary could not believe her eyes.

"Where did all this come from, John dear?" Mary asked when she recovered from the shock.

"I guess you might say the Lord sent it to us. The neighbors and my parents gave it to us for the most part. I made some of it, too," John explained.

John took Mary into his arms and lifted her up, spinning her around and around like a top. Mary squealed and clung to him, her arms about his neck. When he set her down, she jumped up and down for pure delight exclaiming, "Oh, John, I have never been so happy in my whole life!"

# chapter 5

The fall rains brought a slackening in the work at the forge. John was not as busy as he had been in the summer and early fall. After supper, he would often go to the alehouse and remain until late in the evening. Mary complained about this to him, but he shrugged it off usually with some flimsy excuse. "A man wants to be with his friends, Mary, you must understand. When the fall rains stop and the work increases, I will then be home more in the evenings."

One evening late, John came home drunk. He tried to kiss Mary, but she turned away from him in disgust. "Look, John Bunyan, I do not have to live with a drunkard. My father was a godly man. We never had this in our home. Auntie told me, if you were not good to me, I could always come back to her home; and Mr. Morrison will give me my old job back if I need it." Mary was weeping softly.

John was taken by surprise. It was the first time he had seen Mary really angry. He was disturbed deeply and began to apologize.

"I don't want your apologies, I want a sober husband," Mary sobbed. "I love you, John, dearest—you know how much; but I cannot abide a drunkard."

"I promise you, Mary, solemnly and before God, if you will not go away and leave me, I will never be drunk again." John Bunyan kept those solemn words. He knew that he must stay away from the alehouse if he were to avoid its results. From then on he stayed home in the evenings. He never went to the alehouse again. His besetting sin now was playing Sunday games on the Village Green.

When John and Mary were married, Mary brought with her, as her only personal possession from her father, two books—*The Plain Man's Pathway to Heaven*, by Arthur Dent; and *The Practice of Piety*, by Lewis Langely, Bishop of Bangor. She reminded John now and then of her father's godly life and encouraged him to imitate him and become a truly good man.

In the evenings, Mary read to him from these books. In *The Plain Man's Pathway*, there were four characters depicted by the author who conducted dialogues about the heavenly way. The book said that many youths forgot that "we must give account." This "giving account" business at a future judgment bar of God troubled John, as did also the description of an unsaved man in *The Practice of Piety.*

John tried hard to reform himself. He no longer drank. He worked hard, attended church on Sundays, played few games, and had stopped much of his swearing. But inwardly, he was still troubled about the wrath of God, for he was beginning to realize the futility of trying to become righteous in his own strength.

✝ ✝ ✝

One Sunday, the vicar preached a sermon on worldliness and cried out against Sunday games. At dinner, John was so morbid he could hardly enjoy the roast duck which Mary had made especially for him. It was early spring and the Village Green was inviting. John thought surely there could be little harm in a simple game of cat.

"Why are ye so melancholy, John? Did the sermon disturb you today?" Mary pried him.

"It's just that I enjoy my cat games, and the vicar condemns them so heartily," John said solemnly.

"Look, now, the vicar is not your God. If you wish to play a game of cat, go on and play it," Mary said testily.

After dinner, John—encouraged by Mary's words—went to the Village Green and engaged in a game of cat. As he was about to hit the ball the third time around, a voice called to him as if from heaven, saying, "John Bunyan, wilt thou leave thy sins and go to heaven, or keep them and go to hell?" John was shocked and nearly dropped his cat stick.

"What is wrong, Bunyan?" called one of his playing mates.

"Nothing much, I guess," Bunyan replied as he gripped his stick firmly.

"I'm damned anyhow, so I might as well enjoy my sins," John muttered to himself under his breath as he continued to play the game. But he soon finished his course and left the field feeling dejected and sad.

✝ ✝ ✝

John continued to be plagued with the terror of God in his conscience as he thought upon his evil ways, even though he was now trying desperately to reform them.

In this mood, he went one cold December day to repair a roof in the country. When his work was done, his fingers were numb with cold. The old mansion on which he was working had a huge fireplace with a large hearth. Above this stood a stately old mantel and above that a stone slab. When John's fingers were thawed out by the fire, he picked up his tools to go. Just then a thought struck his mind. Taking one sharp tool, he chiseled his name into the stone slab above the mantel—*John Bunyan, 1650.* Then he began thinking. "After I'm gone, someone will notice this name and wonder who John Bunyan was…. *I wonder where my soul will be when a long time from now someone reads these carved words?*"

✚ ✚ ✚

Coming home one day, John found Mary very excited. Word had reached Elstow that the King was being tried for treason by Commons as a common criminal. John was very excited when he heard this, muttering, "Cromwell is going too far this time; they have no right to execute the King, even though they disagree with him," he said.

A few weeks later, a traveler stopped at the Bunyan shop in Elstow. "I saw King Charles executed last week," he said. "It was a frightful sight. The King went to the scaffold very calmly, wearing a black cloak, fine breaches, and even his gloves. Two executioners chopped off his head just outside the Whitehall Banqueting House. Many wept aloud for their King as he died," the man said. Mary shuddered, turned pale and went into Papa Bunyan's house.

"If Oliver Cromwell allowed Commons to do this, then he must have thought it was the right thing to do," John said, dropping his head. "One thing is for sure, future kings will not be so quick to presume that they are above the law."

Prince Charles escaped to France, where he found asylum, but England remained in a state of turmoil. Discontent rumbled throughout the land as Oliver sought to reestablish order.

✚ ✚ ✚

One night, after they had gone to bed, Mary snuggled up to John and said, "Dear, I think I have some wonderful news for you. I hope you will be glad. We are going to have a baby," she whispered tenderly to him. John took her into his arms, kissed her and held her tightly to him, exclaiming, "That's the best news I've heard since you said you'd marry me. Ah, Mary, this means more than ever that I must become a good man. I must not go on any longer as I have been. Please help me to come to know Jesus as my Savior."

"All you need to do is fully trust him, John. He will save you, as I have told you so many, many times."

John knew that Mary did not understand that, for him, it could not be merely a matter of simple faith. There must be some other evidence to convince him that God had heard and answered his prayers.

✠ ✠ ✠

In July 1651, the baby was born. John and Mary rejoiced when they saw its tender form. As the midwife laid a child in Mary's arms, she called to John, "Come, see our new baby girl. What shall we call her?"

"Ah, if I have my way, her name shall be Mary, just as yours is," he said with a radiant smile. He touched the baby tenderly and laughed at how tiny she was. There was much happiness in the home, and many in Elstow rejoiced with the young Bunyans for their new baby.

Several weeks had gone by when, one day, Mary apprehensively asked John, "Have you noticed Mary's eyes? They don't seem to be right. She seems not to see things properly."

John began watching his child and making some simple tests of his own. He passed a red cloth before her eyes. She gave no sign of seeing it at all; His heart sank. They called the doctor and he confirmed their fears—little Mary was *blind*!

✠ ✠ ✠

One day, in the spring of 1652, John was walking along a street in Bedford. All at once a voice broke out near him, "Without God, man is nothing," it said. The words were clear and piercing. John looked this way and that. Then he saw four older women sitting just inside a wall talking and working in the bright sunshine. He stopped and became very quiet, listening.

"If only all men could know God's promises and come to see the love of Christ, that they may be born again in a state of grace, they would be protected from Satan's darts," said the second lady.

"God is a God of holiness and love, and not of vengeance. We should share Him with everyone we can," the third lady said.

John noticed that as they worked at their spinning, knitting, and needlework, these women were very happy. They spoke of the joy of the Lord and the peace of mind which they had in serving Him. He longed for that peace, but he moved on silently without speaking to the women.

For days, John thought about this. He even told Mary of what he had overheard these women say to each other, and she assured him that they spoke the truth. After many days, John returned to Bedford to the same place where he had seen the four ladies. To his great joy, they were there again. Picking up courage, John went directly to them.

"I am John Bunyan, a tinker from Elstow. I heard you some days ago talking about a new birth, and I am come to ask if you can tell me about this new birth," John introduced himself to the group.

Sister Munnes was first to speak. "Everyone must have a new birth. Even the chick, when the egg is laid, is no chick. It is in a shell that must be warmed. Then, with proper care, it hatches forth and becomes a new life. So man dwells in darkness until the light of God shines upon him and brings life."

"I am a mean and wicked man. Can I be quickened and saved?"

"The Bible tells us a man is saved by faith; if he hath no faith, then he is lost," Sister Spencer added.

"Our minister, Brother Gifford, would be glad to talk to ye," Sister Munnes said.

"What is your church, and where do you meet?" John asked.

"It started with twelve people, like the Church of Christ," one sister explained. John soon found that this church included such men as John Eaton, Mayor of Bedford; John Grew, former mayor of the city; and many other fine people, some of whom he knew.

"Come to our services, young man, and feed your soul," Sister Munnes said. Sister Spencer offered to place him on their prayer list.

✠ ✠ ✠

One night, John dreamed that he was in Bedford again and saw the holy and happy women, only this time he saw them over a high wall. He was in a mist of fog and icy coldness, and they were in a large green pasture, where it was sunny and warm. He could not climb over the wall; it was far too high. He could not get through the wall, for there was no entrance. Finally, as he went along the wall, he saw a small hole in it. Looking through this hole, he saw the women in the warm sunshine. The hole was so small that he could barely get his head through it. But after getting his head through, he worked until his whole body was through the wall. Then he came and joined himself to the happy women and the beautiful land and was warm and delighted.

He awoke with a heavy heart, realizing it to be only a dream. "Why," he thought, "do such dreams come only to those who are not able to inherit such blessings? Could it be that I am not among the elect, and therefore, reprobate?" He hoped so much that he might be among the elect and blessed.

In this state of mind, John sought Pastor Gifford. St. John's Church had been founded in the twelfth century, and an ancient hospital had occupied the portion which was now the parsonage where Gifford lived. He talked long and earnestly with Pastor Gifford, always coming away with assurance that God could and would save him, but falling again into doubts before long. Sunday after Sunday, John walked from his home in Elstow to the Bedford meeting. Pastor Gifford's sermons had a powerful effect upon John, and he was blessed in his heart as he listened.

About this time, John had a strange and peculiar premonition which greatly frightened him. Satan came to him and suggested to him, "Sell Christ, even as Judas did. *Sell Him! Sell Him!*"

"No, I will not sell him!" John shouted in retort to Satan. But the thought continued to haunt him.

Greatly perplexed, John returned to the older ladies in Bedford and talked with them more about his state of mind and need of soul. They brought much help to him, quoting to him Scriptures and comforting him that God would forgive and save him.

John was always on the lookout for books, especially older ones which he could afford, that he might find something to cheer his soul. One day, while browsing in a bookshop, he found an English translation of Martin Luther's *Commentary upon the Epistle of St. Paul to the Galatians.* John discovered that Luther, too, had been almost drowned in "blindness, superstition, darkness, and dreams and dregs of Monkish idolatry." But God had set him free; so, surely, God would set him free, too, John thought.

As soon as supper was over, he read the Preface and more, discovering to his soul's satisfaction that there had been others like his case before. "Mary," he exclaimed, "God chose Martin Luther.... He was a sinner such as I. He chose him. He can choose me!"

"This is what I have been trying to help you see, John, dear, for a good while now," Mary said quietly.

"Luther's story sounds as if it might have been written out of my own heart," he fairly shouted.

Night after night, John read from Luther's works. His soul gained much help, but he was a great way off from the kingdom. Luther, too, had been sorely tempted even as John had been. He saw this and felt there was hope for him to be saved even yet.

✠  ✠  ✠

It had now been almost a year that John had struggled with that frightful temptation to sell Christ. Often Satan would renew the attack and always John would fight back, shaking his head sometimes almost violently, as if to try and dislodge such a foolish notion from it. "No, I will not sell Him for ten thousands of thousands. I will not, *I will not!*" he would sometimes shout aloud when he was alone and the temptation came to him.

Early one morning, the old temptation fixed upon him. Satan said, "Sell Christ; *sell Him, sell Him!*"

Exhausted, and not yet fully awake, John gave in under the awful pressure. "Let Him go, if He will," John breathed out, in astonishment to himself.

A terrible gloom of melancholy settled over him. He arose and dressed quickly and went out into the yard of the old Abby Church and fell upon his face. Beating his breast he shouted, "I am Esau; my birthright has been sold for a mess of pottage; it is too late; Christ has gone forever from me. I bade Him go."

John rose from the cold ground. All day he was so miserable he could not work. His mind was in great agitation. "I wish I were dead. I would be better off. I'm lost forever as it is, so why live on?" he muttered to himself.

After a sleepless night, during which he suffered great misery, he rose early and headed for Bedford. The yellow sun had brightened in the deep blue sky when he reached the rectory of Pastor Gifford. Gifford himself let John in the door, greeting him cordially.

John complained to Gifford, "I seem even farther from God than I have ever been, instead of getting any nearer." He explained about the awful thing he had done in letting Christ go from him. Gifford urged him to run to Christ with his burden of sin.

"But the burden upon my back is too heavy for me to run to the cross with it," cried John. "I see the shining light on yonder land, but I have not the faith to embrace it," John said weakly.

His wretchedness continued on through the succeeding night. Mary could not comfort him and wondered if he were on the verge of losing his mind. He sat in melancholy silence and meditated upon these things until she feared he would lose his sanity.

One day, before long, he was in the shop of a good man in Bedford. Suddenly he thought he heard a voice, as if it had been from heaven, saying, "Wast any ever refused justification by the blood of Christ?" It seemed as if an angel had spoken to him the tenderest words of comfort. His heart became at ease; and, for a moment, he felt that surely God had forgiven and saved his soul. Going home and up into his attic room, John tried to pray but found it very difficult to get any words to come out. Still, his mind was made up. "I can but die, and if I must die, then I shall die lying at the feet of Jesus, trusting in Him for His mercy," he said to himself. But soon he again fell into great doubts. He said to an older Christian, "I fear I have committed the sin against the Holy Ghost and am never to be forgiven."

"And so do I," replied the old man, confirming all John's most horrible fears.

Some days later, John was sitting in a shop in Bedford, silently pondering his lost estate. All of a sudden, he heard another voice speaking to him out of nowhere. "This sin is not unto death," the voice said. Connecting this with his notion of having sold Christ, he now knew there was forgiveness. If I take advantage of this, there is hope, he thought.

Great light broke into John's soul there that day; joy flooded his heart. Now he was on the same ground as other sinners—he could be saved. Rushing home to Mary, he explained to her what had happened in the shop and rejoiced that God had been so merciful to him. "Oh, Mary, it is like heaven to feel that God's mercy is offered to my poor sinful soul," he exclaimed.

"Yes, John, it is like heaven; it is the peace of heaven itself. You look so much better. I am so happy for you," she said, taking him into her arms.

"So great is my desire to avenge myself for my heinous sin that, if I had a thousand gallons of blood in my veins, I would give it all for my Christ, who has pardoned me this terrible sin," John cried out with joy. He then went to prayer and prayed, "Oh Lord, the tempter told me it was vain to pray, but I thank Thee that Thou didst not allow him complete power. I thank Thee that the mercy of Christ's blood is sufficient to save my soul. Lord, I shall honor Thee most by believing that Thou canst save my soul. Lord, I would gladly honor Thee by believing that Thou not only canst, but that Thou dost save my soul right now."

Then a voice spoke to him, saying, "Oh man, great is thy faith." Great joy welled up in his soul and he rejoiced in the Lord.

His heart swelled with joy, for the Holy Spirit had not only witnessed to his soul, but now this strange voice which he had heard also confirmed all this. At the end of a long walk in what was known as Bunyan's Field, he came to his home in great peace and tranquillity of mind and heart. The heavy chains of conviction, doubts and fears were fallen off indeed, and he was no longer a prisoner of bondage but a son of the living God. Great joy flooded his soul as he entered his home. "Oh, Mary, rejoice with me, rejoice with me; for I, who was so lost, am now found in Christ Jesus, and I who was so bound by sin's chains am now the Lord's free man!" he exclaimed.

Mary took John into her arms, and they wept upon each other's shoulders for a long time.

Shortly after this, John announced to Mary his desire to move to Bedford, to be baptized and to join Brother Gifford's church. Dazed, but glad for anything which would keep her husband happy in the Lord, Mary agreed—stubbornly holding out, however, for her right to attend the Church of England at Bedford. John, of course, agreed. Soon afterwards, they went to Bedford for the baptism.

# chapter 6

At Bedford, they were met by Brothers Gifford, Eaton, Grew, and Harrington. They went to the inlet from the Ouse River where the baptism was to occur. As John stepped into the water with Brother Gifford, he rejoiced and praised God. When the water reached about their waists, Brother Gifford lowered him under the water. John came forth with lifted hands praising God. There was great joy in his heart. He felt that now his sins were truly and forever washed away, not merely in the water, but in the "blood of the Lamb," of which the water was the symbolic seal.

On their way home, John was quiet for several moments. Then he broke out in praises to God. "Do you know, Mary, Brother Gifford said today I am the nineteenth member he has taken into the church there? Nineteen souls to his credit, besides the many others he may have won to Christ. Christ said one soul was worth the world. Brother Gifford is a wealthy man indeed."

"I like him, John. He is so kind and thoughtful. I think I'd like to attend his church part of the time, once we are moved to Bedford," said Mary earnestly.

✠ ✠ ✠

In April 1654, another daughter was born to Mary and John. Mary's cousin Elizabeth, whose nickname was "Bitsy," came to stay with Mary until she was able to do her work again. They named the baby for Bitsy. She was christened in the Elstow Abby Church with Bitsy as her godmother. John rejoiced greatly a few weeks later when he was sure Elizabeth was not blind.

The year of 1654 also brought many changes in England. The so-called Parliament lost many members from their moving away or from expulsion. The Rump Parliament was succeeded by "the Barebones Parliament," so named after one of its most pious members—a fellow who prayed so much during its sessions that he was nicknamed "Praise God" Barebones. The new Parliament consisted of 400 members from England and thirty members from Scotland and Ireland. Although Royalists and Catholics were excluded from voting rights, this Parliament was closer to a truly free one than had been the case of late. The new favor shown toward the Jews by the Lord Protector Cromwell was remarked about in Bedford among the brethren.

"What about the Quakers?" John Bunyan asked. "They frighten me."

"He is allowing religious liberty for all except the Catholics, whom he does not trust at all," Harrington said.

"The Quakers claim to have an inner light," said Gifford. "I know they live like Christians."

"But is there any other light than the Scriptures? Would it not be idolatrous to follow any other light than Christ?" Bunyan asked. The brethren could not answer his questions. John often thought about the Quakers in the months that followed and wondered what they were really like.

✝ ✝ ✝

After long months of preparation and looking for a suitable house, the Bunyans finally moved to Bedford on the first Saturday in April 1655. They had selected an unfurnished cottage on the edge of the city, far enough from the city drainage ditches so as not to be affected by them. It was a half-timbered cottage with a thatched roof, two chimneys, a dormer window and low gables. From this small dwelling there was a beautiful view of the countryside, toward Newham and the blue hills which rose beyond.

One day John was working in his shop. The August sun was also beating down. In the nearby meadow stood his cow; geese and ducks played about the yard. The children romped and sang. Even blind Mary had learned to know the place so well she could get around without a guide most of the time. John's heart was filled with happiness. What more could one ask? A happy and loving wife, sweet children, a good income and a happy home; besides, Christ filled his life with joy and great peace.

The weeds parted, and down the pathway toward the shop came a familiar figure. It was Colonel Okey. His face was troubled. He now attended the same meeting in Bedford as Bunyan. "John, can you make a pitcher with a small spout sufficient for drinking from?"

"Why, yes, I think so, Colonel. What's the need for it?"

"Pastor Gifford is very sick, and his wife thinks she can get him to drink broth better with this type of pitcher, if it's properly spouted," the colonel explained.

John swallowed hard. "What's the matter with him? Does he know, or have they had a doctor to see him?"

"As a physician, he has diagnosed his own case as consumption."[†]

While John made the pitcher, the two men talked about the good pastor. It was Colonel Okey's opinion that Gifford had used up all his strength on his charge, going day and night, and had about spent his days on earth.

John frowned. "What about Cromwell? How do you feel toward him, since you were relieved of your command sometime ago?"

"John, I regret to speak this way, but the Lord Protector is gaining too much power for his or England's good."

✠ ✠ ✠

John's work increased quickly after he was settled in Bedford. Mary was expecting a third baby and was sick much of the time. John was unable to be as attentive as he had wished to be to his dear pastor, Brother Gifford. When the child was born, he was christened at St. Cuthbert's as John.

A few weeks later, Pastor Gifford died peacefully. The bells of St. John's tolled long and mournfully for his departure to be with Christ. Following a brief funeral sermon, which spoke chiefly of his useful life and future reward, his body was interred in the churchyard at St. John's under a tall elm tree, near the quiet riverside. John wanted to cry out to one and all that their good pastor was not dead but alive forevermore, and even now, walking with Christ in Paradise!

After some debate regarding a successor, the little group appealed to Cromwell himself for aid in selecting a pastor. He sent them a young man of twenty-three, John Burton. Burton assumed his duties in January of the year following Gifford's death, and Bunyan offered his services. "I assisted our former pastor in all ways I could, and I shall be happy to be of service to you, Pastor Burton."

In the following months, John often went into the country at the pastor's request, gathering groups together and speaking to them, praying for the sick and ministering the Word. Sometimes he wished he could

---

† *Consumption* is an old term for tuberculosis of the lungs, or a wasting disease.

stay at home more with his family. "I regret to be away from you and the children, Mary dear, but the Lord is using me."

"Never mind us, John. You must do the Lord's will and work," Mary said. John noticed, however, that she looked very pale at times. But then, this was to be expected. They were expecting their fourth child, and time seemed to pass so quickly.

When the child finally arrived, they christened him Thomas at St. Cuthbert's, after Grandpa Bunyan.

"Four children, two girls and two boys. We are certainly fulfilling the command to be fruitful and multiply, John," Mary said, looking very frail and white.

"I know, and that means I'll have to work harder at the forge." But he could not well do so, for the calls for his services as a minister were now coming so often, he hardly had time for supporting his family. Crowds gathered to hear the "tinker of Bedford." Some called it preaching; others said it was mere ranting and raving.

Colonel Okey needed his roof patched and sent for John one cold February day. As they worked, Okey shouted at John, "Freedom of a proper kind is one thing, John, but the country is filling with these Quakers who have only contempt for the Word of God."

John could hardly believe his ears. "Contempt for the Word of God?"

"Yes, that's exactly what I mean. There is a new group of them springing up who say they have the indwelling Holy Spirit and do not even need the Bible," Okey explained.

After talking with Colonel Okey, John thought much more seriously than ever about the Quakers. He decided that day to do something about this new movement. During the next few days, he talked with a number of people over the countryside who seemed to understand the Quakers. He secured what he thought was adequate information about the Quakers and their beliefs.

"Well, Mary, I'm going to do something I have always wanted to do," John said, as he came into the family room from his study one evening after work. He had a pen and some sheets of paper in his hand.

"You are not going to take up writing are you, dear, on top of all else?"

"That's exactly what I am going to do, my love," he said. That night John Bunyan discovered a secret. When he had an interesting subject and certain convictions of its truth, he could write!

As Mary finished reading his work about the Quakers, she gasped, "Why, John, I never knew you had such talent. What will you do with this? Do you suppose Matthias Cowley would publish it? He doesn't like the Quakers, and you have certainly set people right about their beliefs here."

"I had not even thought of him. Maybe he would print it for us. At least I'll send him a copy and get him to look at it." He wrote the title for the pamphlet, |*Some Gospel Truths Opened,*\and sent it to Crowley.

To John's surprise, Matthias Cowley published the pamphlet. It was read so widely and stirred so much discussion that a young Quaker, Edward Burroughs, made a reply to it the following spring in a pamphlet which "contended for the faith in a spirit of meekness against the opposition of John Bunyan, a professed minister of Bedfordshire."

John soon outlined a reply to Burroughs' treatise and had it ready for the press. He wrote in the white heat of his disturbed spirit, in an amateurish way and with dogmatic conviction and force. And from that first little stream, there began to flow the mighty rolling river of John Bunyan's written works.

# chapter 7

Some time later, John Bunyan completed his second pamphlet about the Quakers, calling it *A Vindication of Gospel Truths Opened*. In this work Bunyan accused the Quakers of being similar to the Ranters. "The Ranters made the doctrines of the Gospel threadbare as an alehouse, and the Quakers have set a new gloss upon them again by an outward holiness."

Mary became alarmed about John's writing so vehemently against the Quakers. One evening at suppertime, she ventured to speak her mind on the subject. "Don't you feel, John, that you can do more for the Lord's cause by positive preaching and writing, rather than by trying to tear down the faith of others? I like the Quakers myself and believe they are harmless. Is it fair for you, who fought for religious freedom, to denounce the Quakers for their use of this freedom?"

John was hit hard by this. It stunned him for Mary, who was always so docile, to take this kind of stand. "I preach positively, Mary, and their doctrine seems to deny the divine nature of Christ; I cannot abide it," he said.

John's pamphlet, *A Vindication of Gospel Truths Opened*, published by Matthias Cowley, sold widely and gave him a reputation as an argumentative preacher and writer. Crowds now flocked to hear him wherever he went to preach. His messages rang out in clear, vibrant tones from village greens, woodland meetings, barns, chapels, and roadways. Many felt convicted of their sins and were converted to Christ. Soon many meetings sprang up in various places where his converts met for worship. For a short while, Bunyan preached against the Quakers. He accused them of legalism and of teaching "salvation by works." He thought of them as a new sect, and therefore, one to be suspected. Their insistence upon the living Christ within and rejection of all sacraments and even of baptism made them an easy target for ecclesiastical criticism.

At length, Bunyan saw that he had a better Gospel to preach. "I have now decided to preach Christ and Him crucified and leave off preaching against others," John said to Mary one day.

For years he had read widely all the books he could afford to buy. He especially appreciated Luther, Knox, and Cromwell. He was greatly influenced by Luther's ideas of freedom of the will, though he held to a form of Knox's Calvinism by this time. He was largely a self-made theologian, swinging somewhere between Luther's free grace for all and Knox's Presbyterianism. He did not so much insist upon doctrines as upon the soul experiencing conversion to God.

One day, it was announced that John would preach at Newport Pagnell on the Village Green. A large crowd flocked to hear him there. Among them was a young man, sent by Matthias Cowley, to bring back a report to him. Just before the appointed hour, John arrived by horseback and hitched his horse to the nearby hitching rail.

John rose to speak and announced as his text, "Repent and be baptized, everyone of you, that your sins may be washed away when the times of refreshing shall come from the presence of the Lord."

For thirty or forty minutes he thundered the Law from Sinai and the Gospel from the New Testament in profound mixture.

"The magistrate may forgive, but it is not the Law that forgives," he cried. "It is unbending, demanding eternal justice from and for all. Only in Christ is there hope for forgiveness.

"When I first began to preach, the terrors of the Law and the guilt of my own conscience lay heavy upon my soul. I was as one sent from the dead to my hearers. I went myself in chains to preach to them in chains. I carried that fire in my own conscience of which I warned my hearers to beware. God carried me on with a strong hand, for neither guilt nor hell could take me off my course as a minister of God to proclaim His eternal truth.

"It was only as I saw that Christ is the hope of all men that this pain in my breast eased and I saw myself forever hidden from the wrath of God in Christ."

The great crowd stood transfixed while Bunyan poured out his soul to them. He had read widely, and his own struggle through the slough of despond and over the hill of difficulty helped him to show others the way. He drew illustrations from his work as a tinker and from many sources of life. He was a fluent speaker, and a persuasive preacher of the Word.

John was opposed to all forms of liturgy. He thundered out, "The formal man-made prayers such as are used by the Anglican Church rise no higher than the head of the vicar and are not more effective than his snoring at night." The great audience guffawed in loud laughter. Smiling, John waited a moment.

He was as stern as John the Baptist. But the people loved it and shouted many an "Amen!" as he preached to them.

He then cried out against the worldliness of believers. "I was trying to be a believer and also a worldling. I played cat on Sundays on the Village Green and drank an occasional ale. I had no real peace of God in my heart."

A few weeks later, Matthias Crowley's quarterly review carried a report of Bunyan's sermon and description of him as Crowley's reporter had brought it back to him:

> John Bunyan, tinker of Bedford, turned minister, preached on the Village Green in Newport the first of last month. He is now a young man of twenty-six, who gave some earlier years of his life in the Parliamentary Army.
>
> Bunyan is a fluent speaker and draws large crowds wherever he goes in the Midlands. He is tall and rawboned, ruddy complexioned and his head is crowned with a shock of reddish brown hair. His eyes are deep blue and very luminous. He has a hearty laugh and is given to much movement in his sermons. His illustrations are very apt and his logic most compelling.

Some time following the Newport sermon, John was to preach in Stevington; but he had been under a shadow lately. His soul was bowed down under the oppression of the enemy, who had tried to instill back into his mind the old doubts about his acceptance of God.

As he walked up the hill toward Stevington, he was very depressed. He felt he had no message for the people that day. He also felt the old load of sin on his back again. He felt so condemned that he knew he could not preach.

As he rose to speak, the cloud settled upon him more heavily, if anything. He tried to speak a few words, but they seemed cold and clammy. He stammered on for several minutes, saying nothing of any consequence.

Seeing the crowd was disappointed, Bunyan said to them in concluding his message. "I am dreadfully sorry to disappoint you as I have today. My own heart is so heavy that I cannot go on. I must retreat to a place alone with my Master for the help of my own soul."

His utter honesty shook the congregation and many offered a handshake of genuine sympathy and appreciation for his words.

As John went back down the hill toward the main road, he felt drained. His heart felt as if it had been turned to stone. "Oh, God, take away this heavy burden of guilt. I have not denied Thy name, nor turned from following Thee. Help Thou me just now," he prayed.

Just then the sun shone out from under a cloud. He turned to gaze at the village cross in the gleaming sunshine. Suddenly he felt as if a huge black burden rolled off his back. He seemed to see it roll down the hillside and into a large spring at the foot of the hill, where it seemed to be washed away. The spring came from the mouth of a cave. At once this cave seemed to represent to John the tomb of Christ, where His body

61

had been laid. John now felt a sense of deep, inner cleansing such as he had not before felt. Until this hour, he had never seen so fully what the atonement of Christ had meant.

✝ ✝ ✝

By August 1658, Bunyan had produced his third book, *A Few Sighs From Hell or the Groans of a Damned Soul*. This volume had wide circulation, adding to the tinker's fame as both preacher and writer.

The national scene was now in an alarming state. George Fox had recently come from London and had published his premonition regarding the Lord Protector's death.

Upon hearing about this in Bedford, John galloped to Ampthill and saw Colonel Okey. Okey said, "Yes, I fear his prophecy will come true. I have a letter from London which says Oliver is dying. The Royalists will probably seize this time to bring Charles back to the throne." Okey looked very dejected.

"What will you do then, if Prince Charles returns, since you were directly implicated in the killing of his father?" John asked a bit shakily.

"That remains to be seen. I will possibly get the block or have to flee the country. Dick Cromwell—you know Richard, Tumbledown they call him—will probably be named the Lord Protector to succeed his father, but he's a weakling and will not last long. Then it's anybody's guess what will happen."

On September 3, the anniversary of the victories of the Parliamentary Army at Dunbar and Worcester, Oliver Cromwell died. News of his death spread a pall of gloom over most of England.

Hardly anyone in Bedford was more deeply moved and grieved than John Bunyan. Oliver Cromwell had been his friend since the day they fished together, and Cromwell had saved his life. What a king had not been able to do, Cromwell had done—subdued Scotland and Ireland and made England a powerful nation. Would Prince Charles now be brought back to England? These thoughts beset Bunyan's mind.

Mary tried to comfort him. "John, dear, God still lives; we must rely on Him, even if the great Lord Protector is dead."

"I know, Mary, but oftentimes God does not seem to have His way in the affairs of men."

That evening they ate in silence, save for the children's remarks. Mary went to the kitchen and washed the supper dishes, then she came into the family room and lay down on the couch. John soon came and took her hand in his and sat a long time holding it. Feeling her forehead, he realized that she had a fever. "Do you have these fevers very often, my dear?" he asked.

"Oh, now and then I get one, but I'll be all right. I just need a good night of rest. The children and the housework are so demanding at times. Lately you have been so busy you have had little time to help with anything, not even with correcting the children." Her voice seemed far away.

"Yes, darling, I know. I've been gone far too much. I shall try to stay closer to home. I must stay by the forge more, too, if we are to be prepared for another winter," John said.

✠ ✠ ✠

About a month later, John came home from a trip he had made and found Mary in bed. John went for Dr. Banister. He was getting old now and seldom made night calls, but for Mary's sake he came. After examining her the doctor looked very grave. "She's a sick girl, John, very sick. I'm not sure what we can do for her, but we'll have to try the remedies."

"What seems to be the ailment?" John asked.

"Quick consumption, I fear, my boy," Dr. Banister said as he left the house.

John went to Mary's room and placed his arms about her. She broke into tears. John held her tenderly in his arms and kissed her cheeks over and over, mingling his tears with hers.

"Oh, surely the Lord would not take you away from me now when I need you so very, very much. I am giving my all to His work. Surely, Mary, He will help you."

Two days later, Dr. Banister returned. Later, when he came from the room, he said to John, "Doesn't look as if there is anything further I can do. I have given her all the remedies I know and she does not seem to rally. It is doubtful whether she will last through another night."

John went to Mary's bed, which had now been moved into the family room.

"What did he say, John? Tell me all. I know I must soon go to be with Christ. It will not worry me."

Great tears rolled down John's ruddy face. He lifted her into his strong arms and held her frail body close to his as he sat on the bed. She was hot with fever. "Darling, he said you are very sick, and that you may not last much longer."

"I expect no miracle, John. I shall soon be safely home in the happy hills of God. I regret to leave you, dear, but God will provide for you and the children." John thought he had never seen her more beautiful since their wedding day. He deeply regretted that he had been gone so much and had left her with so many responsibilities—even to the copying and correcting of his manuscripts for the books he had written.

"When will cousin Bitsy come?" Mary asked.

"She should be here yet tonight," John said.

The following day Mary sank into unconsciousness, lingering in this stage all that day and the next. She often mumbled, but no one could understand her. As John sat by her side late in the afternoon, she rallied and looked at him with tender compassion. "Oh, John, the delectable mountains I have been seeing are most wondrous. I wish you could see them. I know you could write most beautifully about them if you only saw them!" Mary exclaimed. Mary closed her eyes and was silent for a long time. John wept bitterly as he held her thin hand in his large, rough one. Once she rallied a little and her large, beautiful brown eyes rested on John for a moment. A tiny smile played about her lips, then she closed her eyes. Soon all signs of life had gone. John laid her hands across each other over her chest. "Good-bye, my darling, till we see each other again on those delectable mountains, beyond this vale of tears."

Two days later, the funeral service was read in St. Cuthbert's Church. The plain wooden box containing Mary's earthly remains was lowered into the sod under the twisted limbs of an old tree in the churchyard.

John slept little that night. He had had a hard time getting little Mary to go to bed. The poor blind child could not understand where her mother had gone, though she was now eight years old. She had never experienced death in the home. The other three children were cared for by Bitsy, who had remained to help John with things for a few days.

✠ ✠ ✠

The Bedford Church ladies were most gracious to John in the months that followed. Often different ones would take turns house-cleaning and attending to the children when he was away preaching. Of all the children, he was most anxious about his dear blind Mary. He spent many hours reading to her and holding her on his lap, thus she came to know most of the great Bible stories by heart and many songs and poems. Mary was never more content than in her father's presence or helping him with some piece of work. Her delicate hands could often find pieces of metal or tools which he needed when in the shop or at the forge.

"Why don't ye marry again, John?" Mama Anne said to him one day. "It will soon be a year and ye need someone here to help you care for these little ones and to cook and make a home for ye," she said, looking at John squarely to see how the suggestion set with him.

"There's never been anyone who can take Mary's place. I just don't seem to see anyone I'm that much interested in."

"Maybe not now, but there will be in time," Anne said. She dropped the subject at that.

✜ ✜ ✜

There were many lonely days for John. At times Anne's words would return to him. His thoughts roamed to the younger women he knew, and not one of them seemed to appeal to him as a suitable wife and mother for the children, especially poor little blind Mary.

One day early in June, John looked up the pathway from his shop to the house. To his surprise, he saw a young lady coming toward the shop. John continued to hammer. A moment later the girl entered the shop, pulling off her large hat and calling out to him cheerily, "Hello, Cousin John. I've been thinking a lot about you and the children of late, so I just thought I'd drop in and see how you are doing."

"Bitsy, if it isn't you, bless your dear heart! Girl, I didn't even recognize you with that big sun hat on," John replied, smiling at her.

"Uncle Matthias Cowley brought me over from Newport this afternoon. He is here on some kind of business and will be going back tomorrow." Bitsy tossed her hair back off her shoulders with her hand.

"Oh, then you can spend the night with us. That will be wonderful. And you can see my new manuscript tonight. Can you stay with us? If you can, I'll stop now and we'll go to the house and start something for supper."

"Yes, I came with this in mind, if you think it's all right, Cousin John. If not, I can stay at the inn in town." Bitsy looked into John's eyes to see if he really approved of her staying. She was a bit shy and did not wish to embarrass him.

"Of course you are going to stay," insisted Bunyan.

They walked to the house together. Bitsy soon found the children and got reacquainted with them. Mary, of course, remembered her well and so did John, but Thomas and Elizabeth had forgotten her. Soon Mary was snuggled up against her, telling her some of the Bible stories she had learned, while John busied himself getting the supper meal started. Meanwhile, Elizabeth had made up with Bitsy and was sitting on her lap perfectly contented. Thomas was tugging at her skirt, and John sat admiring her as she talked to Mary about her trip from Newport Pagnell by stagecoach.

"All right. It's ready, if you can stand the old man's cooking, child."

They ate supper amidst the chatter of the children. When the meal was over, Bitsy said, "It's only right that I wash the dishes. After all, I'm not a stranger here." John thought how good it seemed to have a woman in the house again, even if she was but a teenage girl.

After supper, John invited Bitsy to come into the library and see his manuscript. He removed it from the desk drawer. Bitsy sat on the arm of his large desk chair. There were many notes in the margins of the manuscript, and in a number of places lines were crossed out, and other lines were written underneath them in smaller letters.

"What will this one be called?" Bitsy wanted to know.

"I don't know yet, Bitsy. Sometimes I start working on a book, and then I get tired of it and lay it down for awhile till I gather more information—and a bit more inspiration, too. Then I write some more. Sometimes the book gets a different name when it's finished. Do you think maybe you could read this handwriting and recopy this work for me, if you had the time?"

"Of course I can. I can read every word of it. You write with a very legible hand." Just then Bitsy threw back her head and laughed, touching John's shoulder lightly. John felt the touch and flinched. He hoped Bitsy did not notice that he had been aware of it. After all, to her he was only someone close of kin.

John placed the manuscript in the desk and they returned to the family room. "When the manuscript is done, maybe I'll let you do the copy work for me," he said as they reentered the family room.

"Oh, please do, Cousin. I cannot think of anything I would rather do," Bitsy said. Joyfully, John saw the admiration in her eyes. "Just think, if I go on to school and make a good scholar, some day perhaps we can put out a new book by John Bunyan and Elizabeth Bently! How would that strike you?"

When Bitsy was ready to go the next morning, she kissed all the children good-bye and then extended her hand to John, smilingly. "Uncle Matthias has to come back in about three weeks. If I'm not too busy maybe I can come over again."

A sudden urge came over John to take her into his arms. Her deep blue eyes danced with such lively delight. The golden locks of hair were neatly in place. Her forehead was high and her nose slender and almost pointed, turning up the least bit at the end. If Bitsy was aware of any stirrings in John, she did not manifest it. Slowly he released his grip on her hand.

"We wish you could come and stay with us, Bitsy," Mary called out.

"Yes, we do," chimed in young John, clapping his little hands in delight and clinging to her skirt.

"They all love you so much; you are such a comfort to them," John said, heading off their remarks.

The next day, the children all remarked about how much they missed Bitsy. John drew a deep breath at the thought of the tender girl's age and features. "If she were older, I'd ask her to come and stay." His voice sounded strange to him. "I'd be doing just what my father did when he married Anne. It would be disrespectful to my darling Mary," he mumbled to himself. John put the thought out of his mind as he headed for work at the forge.

✝ ✝ ✝

News from London soon took John's attention from everything. Tumbledown Dick Cromwell, as many of the Royalists mockingly called him, resigned from the Lord Protectorship and moved into the country. Soon a strong movement arose to bring back Prince Charles. General Monk, who had served under Cromwell in Scotland, volunteered to command an army to protect him.

In Bedfordshire, William Vierney, the old schoolmaster, offered his services to the Council and was appointed a councilman. All over the country there was general talk that Prince Charles might return, at least within a year. John had several preaching engagements but avoided all reference to the political situation.

One afternoon, as he worked at the forge, he glanced up and who should be coming but the girl with the wide-brimmed hat, Bitsy! "Surprised to see me, Cousin? Do you have the manuscript done for the new book?" she asked, her eyes dancing.

"How fast do you think I can write, girl? It's hard work you must understand," John laughingly replied. "How long can you stay this time, Bitsy?"

"Three days, if you don't mind. Uncle Matthias has gone to London."

"Fine, then maybe we will have some time to work on the book, after all. I thought maybe you were just staying for the night, as before."

Just to have her there with the children would be a great relief. He had a preaching appointment for the middle evening of her stay, and now he would not need to ask a neighbor to stay with the children.

"Now look, young lady," John laughed, "if you are going to stay with us for three days, I'll give you a chance to prove your hand at cooking."

"Let me change dresses," Bitsy said. Then she disappeared into the sleeping chamber, reappearing shortly in a crisp house dress. John thought she looked at least a year older than he remembered her looking the last time she was there.

On the way to market to buy some meat for supper, John thought he would like to speak to Bitsy about staying with them and helping with the children and the chores, but that would never do. People would soon say he kept a mistress, and his influence and ministry would be ruined. He dismissed the thought from his mind.

The next evening, John filled his engagement in the country. When he returned the children were all in bed and Bitsy was reading his manuscript. She had made a copy of the first few pages and showed it to John. "Fine work, my dear little lady, fine work. You would make a most excellent secretary for me if you lived nearby."

"Oh, I'd love to do it, Cousin John. I would get so much help for my own soul from your wonderful writings." She smiled up at him.

John touched her hair lightly, commenting on how beautifully she had done it. She drew back as if he had done the wrong thing. "I'm sorry, Bitsy, I didn't think, I guess. You are so much like one of the family."

He knew his heart was getting the better of him. "Dear Lord, here is a situation in which Thou must intervene. I am weak, Lord. Thou art the only one who canst now help me," he prayed as they returned from the library to the family room.

"Would you marry again, Cousin John, if you found the right person?" Bitsy asked as soon as he was seated beside her on the large couch. John almost gritted his teeth. It took him a moment to get his composure.

"Why, I guess I might consider it, Bitsy, if I knew it would work out all right. I miss Mary so much. Sometimes I'm so sad and feel all alone. Often I just go to my bed and weep out my heart to God, for there is no one else to go to, you see. I guess I really need someone here, but it's hard to get used to the thought of anyone else other than my dear sweet Mary."

"It must be hard for you, Cousin John. I often think of how lonely you are, and I've many times prayed for you," she said, smiling into his eyes.

John felt that he needed extra strength just then as he looked into Bitsy's beautiful face, wreathed with her golden curls.

Turning around on the couch so that he faced her fully, John said, "Bitsy, maybe you will think I'm just a fool, but I cannot wait any longer to express to you some of my thoughts recently. I have been thinking much about you of late. If there were not so much difference in our ages, I don't know of anyone on earth I'd rather have to live here with me for all time to come than you." He looked deeply into her eyes. She sat very still for a long moment.

"You surprise me, Cousin John, really, you do. How could you think such thoughts of me?"

John sat motionless. He knew then he must have said the wrong thing. His tongue seemed as thick as an elephant's hide. He looked at her and felt a deep pain stab his heart.

"I'm sorry, Bitsy dear, if I have hurt you. I guess I've just been a dunce since Mary left me." Tears welled up in his eyes. Bitsy moved closer to him and took his large hand into hers.

"No, John, never! I didn't mean it that way. I meant how could you ever have such sweet thoughts about a poor unworthy young girl such as I, when you are so great and so wonderful, and you need someone strong and able to help you?" Her eyes held his steadily. His heart now felt much lighter. Maybe he had not done too badly after all.

After a long moment of silence, during which Bitsy slowly released his hand, John said, "Bitsy, dear, could you ever consent to be my wife? I know there is a wide age gap, but then you fit in here so perfectly with the children and I must think of them. But more than that, you fit into my very heart, too." He looked at her for a moment and noticed that her cheeks were flushed.

"Perhaps it sounds silly of me, but ever since the first time I was here, I've been praying that, if it was God's will, He would speak to you about this. I've always admired you so much. I love the children and admire your work, and I am in full accord with your religious convictions and beliefs. As for age, what is that? It is love and understanding between a man and his wife that really counts for the most, isn't it?"

John took her slender hand. "Oh, Bitsy, Bitsy, you do not know how very happy you make me. I had not planned to speak to you, but my heart simply couldn't wait any longer, though my head seemed to tell me differently. But I'm glad I obeyed my heart this time."

Looking up into his deep blue eyes and patting his cheeks, Bitsy said, "Well, I guess I shall not be calling you 'Cousin' any more, or shall I?" She laughed softly and laid her head upon his broad shoulder.

A little while later John asked, "When do you wish us to be married? I guess this little detail will have to be attended to before you come for good!" He laughed heartily, holding her hands in his.

"What about three weeks from now?"

Early the next morning, Bitsy was down at the tinker's shop. "Uncle Matthias was to pick me up about nine or ten o'clock. Is there anything I can do here before I go?" she asked.

"Nothing, but look around and see what changes you wish made in things here, before you come," responded the happy tinker.

"Where shall we be married, John? I have no relatives living, you know, but Uncle Matthias."

"Where do you wish to be married, dear?"

"I'd as soon be married at St. Cuthbert's as anywhere. Uncle Matthias can bring me over on the appointed Saturday morning, and we can be married that afternoon. Does this suit you?"

"Couldn't please me better," John said, as they walked toward the house.

Bitsy dressed and fed the children. They had family prayers together. John went into the library and brought out a gold-tipped writing pen. Handing it to Bitsy he said, "This is all I have to give you, dear, in token of our pledges, but it is a symbol of some of the work to which you may be looking forward for yourself." John chuckled merrily.

The next Sunday the bans were published in St. Cuthbert's, and on the appointed Saturday Uncle Matthias brought Bitsy to Bedford for the wedding.

At two o'clock in the afternoon, a large crowd gathered at St. Cuthbert's to see John and Bitsy married.

The old vicar read the service in singsong fashion and was not too well-dressed himself. In his careless fashion, he even forgot to make a notation of the wedding in the register of St. Cuthbert's. John was one of the happiest men in the English Midlands as he and Bitsy drove away for their honeymoon in a carriage he had rented for the occasion.

Back at home several days later, John carried Bitsy across the threshold into her new home. Bitsy was never so happy in her life. She had been an orphan since childhood. Now she had a home of her own. She felt like she imagined how the queen feels when she moves into Buckingham Palace.

John was now very happy and contented. His mind was at ease about the children, and he turned his thoughts more and more to preaching and writing about God's Word. Bitsy carefully copied the notes he had left on bits of paper and arranged them for him on his desk. He would then work them into manuscript form, with his corrections, and she would faithfully recopy them as the final drafts of his manuscripts. John and Bitsy worked steadily that fall on John's new book. When it was ready, Matthias Cowley published it.

As people read *The Doctrine of Law and Grace Unfolded,* many remarked about how John had grown in his writing since his first little book was published. His writings were now much calmer and not so frenzied and harsh. There was considerably more of the love of God in this book than in any other so far. Hundreds were stirred by this book, and it left a lasting influence.

# chapter 8

The fall months glided by quickly. John was busy preaching and working. His writing was a bit more limited at this time, but Bitsy faithfully kept up with what he did.

Christmas came almost before the Bunyans were ready for it. John never liked a lot of toys on Christmas, but they did have a lovely dinner and Bitsy had managed to buy a few presents the children needed.

On Christmas day, John preached at Yelden at William Dell's church. The service went well. Reports of it went far around the countryside.

On the political front, the Royalists were gaining ground everywhere in England. Older Puritans were being thrown out of office and were being replaced with Royalists. Freedom for the Puritans and even the Presbyterians was drying up like a fountain in the heat of summer.

John said to Bitsy one evening after supper, "I hear there are rumblings of discontent about my preaching in William Dell's church Christmas day. The government is clamping down on preachers who do not have a state license issued by the Anglican Church. Even some of the Presbyterians frown on unlicensed preachers, especially among the Puritans. While I am not strictly a 'Puritan,' yet I am so classed, because the Meeters are not a church the government recognizes, and our ministers are not government-licensed."

"What will happen then, John, if you continue to preach without a license? Will they imprison you? What would I and the children do, if they did?" Bitsy was plainly worried.

"Never mind, let's not cross bridges till we reach them, dear. It's not too late for God to work miracles. We will just wait and see," John comforted Bitsy.

✟ ✟ ✟

Early in February, word was circulated that Thomas Becke, an Anglican minister of the area, was going to have John arrested for preaching without a license, John thought little of it, until one day an officer appeared at his door. "You are under arrest for preaching without a license at a farmhouse near Lowell Samuel this past October," said the officer.

"Wait a minute, now, officer. Where did you get your authority for this?" John asked, unbelievingly. "I cannot believe my ears. Did we not fight for this freedom? Has the government changed form so soon as this? Where is your authority?"

"Sir, you will have to ask the justice this. We simply have orders to arrest you. That's all I know about it. You are to appear with me at the court today. I am sorry, but you will have to come with me."

Bitsy broke into tears. "Oh, John, whatever will I do with the children? Will you be imprisoned? When will you be home again?" she sobbed.

"I don't know, dearest. All I know now is what you heard the officer say. I will try to work something out. I hope there will be no imprisonment. I see no reason for this. Possibly there is some misunderstanding."

John went with the officer. At the court hearing, William Dell appeared and vindicated John. He had known of his earlier preaching. Moreover, he had also invited John to preach for him Christmas day in his own pulpit. Becke withdrew his charges and John was freed and returned home a happy man.

✠ ✠ ✠

That spring, Parliament voted to bring Prince Charles back from exile. At the end of April, emissaries were sent to Bruges with sufficient funds for the triumphant return of the monarch.

John worried about what might happen to Colonel Okey. He rode to see him, finding him very dejected and sad. He had married again a young bride and did not wish to leave her, but flight to Europe or somewhere was his only sure hope of saving his life. Colonel Okey said, "I fear I shall have to leave England. I see no other chance of survival."

The days wore away toward the twenty-ninth, Prince Charles's thirtieth birthday. On that sunny day, he rode into London. In anticipation of his coming coronation, he had been welcomed at Dover with flying colors and triumphant shouts of "*God save the King!*" Hundreds gathered along the roadway to sing his praises and welcome him back to the kingdom and to his throne.

The reign of Oliver Cromwell, with its high morality and strictness, was at an end; England would once more become "merry old England."

That night, after dark, bonfires were lighted about London, and many alehouses served free liquor.

Almost as soon as he was crowned, King Charles started carousing and neglecting affairs of state. Chancellor Hyde ran the kingdom. An order for the arrest of Colonel Okey, who had assisted in the assassination of King Charles I, was now issued. Okey fled to the Continent. To show contempt for Cromwell and his work, a mob exhumed, hanged, and then buried the bodies of Cromwell, his son-in-law Ireton, and John Bradshaw in unmarked graves.

The Presbyterians in Parliament, in their haste for Charles's return, had failed to secure from him any exact promises and had imposed no conditions. This gave Charles a free hand. Chancellor Hyde pursued the policies of Charles I and was determined to throttle the consciences of all the people where possible, restricting all but Anglicans from freedom of worship.

✠ ✠ ✠

The next year, September 13 to November 1, the Quarter Sessions at Bedford ordered the general use for all Anglican Churches of the Liturgy and the Book of Common Prayer.

One cold November evening, as the Bunyan children were listening to John and Bitsy recite verses and tell stories, there came a knock at the door. John answered the door. There stood Paul Cobb, the local constable in charge of Bedford county and city jails. "Come in, my good man, come in," John said in his usual good-natured tone.

Cobb looked very serious as John offered him a chair. "Is there trouble brewing, Cobb?" Bunyan asked.

"Well, there's something we should discuss, at least, John," Cobb said. "Ye'd best stick to soldering pots and pans instead of trying to save souls in meetings from now onward for awhile, John."

"What's the problem, Cobb?"

"Under the new government being run by Chancellor Hyde, the laws which forbid unlicensed preachers to preach will be enforced, we have been warned. Ye could get yourself into trouble, John."

John straightened up in his chair to his full height. "Did Foster send you here to tell me this?" John said crisply.

"It's my job, John, to enforce the laws. I just thought I'd tell ye in advance. It's not that I'd *want* to do such a thing, but I'd have no choice if ye broke the laws about this."

"I will go on mending pots and kettles weekdays and saving souls at nights and on Sundays," John said.

"This is fair warning, John. Many Puritan preachers have left their pulpits and some have fled the country," Cobb explained.

"I'm not fleeing the country, nor am I ceasing to preach."

"I realize that, but Bunyan, don't be a fool. You know how the Wingates feel about the Meeters. Anne Wingate is William Foster's wife, and Francis, who is her brother, is the Justice at Harlington."

"Yes, I know. The Wingates suffered during the war for their Royalist sympathies. Now, they are in power and would doubtless make it hard on any Puritan, especially those who fought on the other side of the war." John thought for a moment. "I've heard there's a hiding hole for Royalists under the gables of the old Harlington House," John laughed.

"This is not a funny matter, John. The tide has turned. The Fosters and Wingates will search out all the unlicensed preachers and close every conventicle and Meeters Meeting in the country. The cost of disobeying the law will be imprisonment or banishment for all those caught," Paul Cobb warned Bunyan.

"God will take care of me so long as I am doing His will," John said with firmness and conviction.

After Paul left, John sat staring into the fire.

The Restoration Act had taken freedom away. Immorality was sweeping the country. It was common knowledge that Charles kept a succession of mistresses and had a number of illegitimate children. Everywhere, prostitution and adultery reigned with a loose hand. In such an hour, how could he promise not to preach the Gospel of Christ? He would never do it!

John made up his mind as he sat by the fireside and mused that cold November in his Bedford home. "If it means imprisonment for preaching the Gospel, Bitsy," John said when she came from putting the children to bed, "it will just have to mean that. I cannot defile my conscience, when God has done so much for me, by withholding the Word of life to others just because a corrupt government says I cannot preach without a license." John stood up before the fire, stretching himself to his full height.

"But John, dearest, what will happen to the children and me? You know that I am with child and am expecting to be delivered in a few weeks. What if you are not even here to welcome his coming?" Bitsy stood and placed her arms about John's neck and laid her head on his shoulder. She patted his cheek—a way of expressing her tender affection.

75

He took her into his arms and they stood silently for a moment. The fire crackled in the fireplace. John swallowed hard, as he usually did when something was agitating him. "Bitsy, my darling, if I must suffer the persecution of imprisonment for Christ's sake, even as Paul of old, will not our Lord take care of you and the children? I am sorry for you, dearest, so young and tender; and I love you so very, very much." He held her tightly and kissed her. Then he broke into great heaving sobs. Tears rolled down his face. "Oh God, do Thou strengthen me in this hour."

Bitsy kissed John on the cheek. "Let us not worry, dearest; who knows, the Lord may turn this evil tide, and you may yet be able to go on with your ministry unhampered. Bedford Meeting is a recognized church, isn't it?"

"Yes, by the public, but not by the government. With the government, we are in the same case as the Independents, the Quakers, and the Puritans."

"I'll stand by you, whatever comes, John, dear, you know that," Bitsy said.

# chapter 9

One morning shortly after this event, while Bunyan worked in his shop, a sealed note was delivered to him by a special messenger. Upon opening it he found that Farmer Burgess, at Lowell Samuel, had requested that he preach to a small congregation on Sunday morning, the twelfth of November. Bunyan scribbled his reply that he would be there at the appointed time, resealed the note and gave it to the messenger boy, who returned it to the farmer. Farmer Burgess was in Bedford on business.

Early Sunday morning on the twelfth, John kissed Bitsy good-bye and rode off for his meeting at Lowell Samuel. It was a small village about one mile from Harlington Church and near the home of the widely known justice, Francis Wingate. It was a cold day and John spurred his horse onward, reaching the farmhouse about ten o'clock. A small crowd had already gathered and they greeted Bunyan cheerily upon his arrival. He noticed, however, that several looked at each other curiously despite the cheery greetings.

Farmer Burgess asked to see Bunyan in the kitchen of the home. "I must tell you, Brother Bunyan, that a warrant has just been issued for you, if you conduct a service here today; and the constable has been ordered to watch the house. Justice Wingate seems determined to get you into trouble."

John thought again of all the happy days he had had with Bitsy and the children. His resolve was firm and his mind made up. He would not allow the cross of Christ to be dragged in the mud of cowardice and compromise.

"What's your decision, John?" said Farmer Burgess at length.

"If we run like mice, how can we witness our beliefs?" John said. "No, I shall not call off the meeting. We will go ahead with it."

Several songs were sung and John had read a Scripture lesson and was ready to speak when a resounding knock sounded on the door. Farmer

Burgess went to the door, trembling as he opened it. In walked the constable and two others of Wingate's men. "Are you John Bunyan, and are you conducting a service here?" the constable asked, looking John in the face.

"I am, sir, and we are having a Gospel worship service."

"Then I have a warrant for your arrest. I must ask that you come with me now and desist from this service. Magistrate Wingate has issued the warrant and I am serving it in his name."

John followed the men to the door. Looking back from the doorway, he said to the congregation, "Don't look so downcast. It is better to be persecuted than to persecute.... Freedom's dead in England."

John mounted his horse and followed the men. They came to the old Harlington House, which was located on the corner of the crossroads, near the historic old church. The old house was elegant. It had stood there for a long time. Two huge pilasters[†] looked as if they held up the red-tiled roof. There were five dormer windows across the top in the upper story. Looking at this great sprawling structure, John remembered that his father had told him once this house dated back to at least 1396, maybe even further back. They entered the great parlor where the meeting was to take place. It was a large oak-paneled room. A polished desk sat in one corner with papers neatly arranged lying on the corner of the desk. Behind the desk sat Justice Wingate in a black robe. He had been born the same year as Bunyan, but his hair was graying and deep lines etched his face. He had suffered, too, during the war. Maybe, after all, he does not wish to be unkind, John thought.

Wingate looked at John for a fleeting moment, then turned to the constable. "What evidence did you find at the farmhouse?" he asked.

"Your Honor, I present the tinker preacher arrested on your orders. We found no evidence of treason against the government, no weapons of any kind and no papers that would incriminate him. The tinker was merely conducting a gospel service."

"The Conventicle Act provides that there shall be no gathering of any more than five persons for any kind of worship, other than the family, and at any place besides the authorized parish church," Wingate said as he tapped on the desk with his fingers.

"But this man meant no harm, I can assure you, Your Honor," the constable said. "He and the small crowd were perfectly peaceable," the constable explained.

---

† A *pilaster* is a mock column that protrudes slightly from the wall of a building; it usually has a simulated capital and base.

"He has broken the law! The punishment calls for an imprisonment of three months unless he does penance and promises publicly not to preach nor convene a crowd again. If he does break it, he could be hanged or banished," Wingate said, his cold black eyes resting on John.

John stepped forward a little. "I went to the farmhouse only to preach the Gospel of Christ," he said.

"Why can't you attend to your tinkering, John Bunyan? Why do you have to break the law?" Wingate snapped.

"God's tinker mends souls as well as pots and pans, sir," Bunyan said.

"I shall break the neck of these meetings!" Wingate said angrily.

"Perhaps," John replied quietly.

Wingate pounded the desk furiously. "Since you take such a stubborn stand and will persist in it, we shall make you an example for other Meeters. You shall go to prison for three months," Wingate said.

While Wingate was preparing the writ, John waited in the hall. In a few minutes the door opened and in stepped a huge man wearing a vicar's garb. John recognized him instantly as Dr. William Lindall, a curate, who was married to one of Wingate's relatives. His eyes rested on John and he said, "Well, well, what are you doing here, John Bunyan?"

"I am here because I held a meeting yesterday to pray, read the Scriptures, and preach."

"You had no right to be doing this, you know, according to the laws of the land," Lindall said.

St. Peter's words flashed into John's mind. "'As every man hath received the gift, even so let him minister the same,' St. Peter said. I was only carrying out this word," John replied.

"There was a coppersmith who did St. Paul much evil; do you remember him?" Lindall said as he started to go on into the house.

Bunyan remained silent for a moment. "I remember the Pharisees, too, who spilled our Lord's blood," he blurted out at Lindall.

Lindall was taken by surprise at these words and walked on toward the room at the end of the hallway. "That old enemy of God!" Bunyan thought. He felt like shouting after him, "Answer not a fool according to his folly," but he thought better of it and said nothing more.

Soon Wingate returned with the documents drawn up for John's imprisonment. He handed them to the constable and told him to deliver John to the Bedford jailer. He did not speak again to John. Just as the constable and John were leaving the mansion, they were met by two men from Bedford. News of John's arrest had reached Bedford early that morning. Mayor Grew and a Mr. Harrington had ridden into Harlington to see what could be done for him.

"Let us return to Wingate. I know him well. I believe we can arrange for a change in this affair," Grew said.

"I think it useless to return, but if the constable is willing, I am willing to try for it," John said quietly.

The four men returned to the Wingate mansion. On the way, John prayed for grace and strength. The serving man led the four men into the parlor. Soon Francis Wingate appeared again. The Bedford men made known their business, and Wingate asked them to come with him into an inner office. It seemed like a long time before they appeared again in the hearing room. "The justice says he will release you, if you agree not to do anything to endanger the King's authority," Mr. Harrington said.

"The King's or Chancellor Hyde's?" John asked.

"If you say certain words, it will be all right, John," Grew said.

"Only if the words are not against my conscience will I say them," John answered.

Wingate asked John to come into his office in the inner room. Waiting there were Dr. Lindall and William Foster, avowed enemies of the Bedford Meeters' Meeting. Foster was first to speak. "John, consider well what you are doing today. Do not make a fool of yourself. I am here to help you."

"What do you want me to do?"

"Dr. Lindall and I have been discussing your case with Wingate. No one wants to send you to prison," Foster said in words as smooth as butter.

"Tell me what I have done that is wrong," said John.

"How can it possibly be lawful for an ignorant tinker like you to preach the Gospel without any license?" Foster asked.

For a moment all stood in silence. Foster looked at John, standing tall and erect. He knew that John Bunyan would never bend or compromise for anyone. The look of sturdy determination glistened in John's eyes. It was this quality of absolute sincerity and uncompromising leadership which gave Bunyan's messages the powerful force which they had. "England has too few such men now," Foster thought, as he waited for Bunyan to speak.

"As Peter of old, I must obey God rather than man, in this case. I must tell others about the Lord Jesus Christ," John returned in a firm strong voice. "What is wrong with that?"

"There is nothing left to do but to carry out the writ. Take him to Bedford jail and hold him there without bond until the Quarter Sessions in January," Wingate said curtly. "That is all we can do with this stubborn tinker."

✠ ✠ ✠

"I am bothered most about Bitsy and the children," John said to Grew as they rode toward Bedford. "I know not how I shall be able to support them in prison, but surely the Lord will care for them."

"Don't worry about that, John. We will see that they are cared for. There are many people in Bedford who believe in your ministry who will see that they shall not go uncared-for," Grew promised him.

The little old jail in Bedford was on the bridge over the Ouse River. It was part of the much larger grain toll house where tolls were collected from river boats which carried foodstuffs to London from the North Midlands country. There was room for only about eight or ten persons in the jail and there were generally fewer than this in it.

The deputy jailer who was in charge of prisoners was Paul White, an old companion of John's in army days at Newport Pagnell. "John, I'm sorry to see you here. We heard late last night about the bad news of your arrest, but we were hoping Grew and Harrington could get you off without a sentence here," Paul said as he admitted John that night.

"Wingate was adamant," John explained. "He would not release me on any condition other than that I promise not to preach again. Paul, you know me, you know I could never be free in my spirit if I made and kept such a promise as this."

"I know, John. We'll just make the best of it here till the Quarter Sessions. I'll get some new bedding tomorrow and you can have the best we have here, you know that."

"Thank you, Paul. Try to get word to my wife tonight that I am here and safe, will you?"

"I'll surely see that she gets the word, John," Paul said as he left him.

John stared for a long time after Paul left at the silent stars far away in the sky. There was a small window in the room which opened toward the river. He heard the waters gurgling as they washed against the huge posts supporting the river bridge. Bitsy and the children would have no means of support. It was winter and they had provisions to last only a few weeks, but there was no lien against the house so there was no danger that they would be moved out into the cold. He was glad for that, and Bitsy did know how to make laces of leather for the men's boots, and

81

they sold well. Possibly she could get some support in this way, he thought.

✝ ✝ ✝

The next morning, Bitsy came to the jail to see John. Her eyes were red from weeping, and she said she had not slept much the night before. Paul White had come over around midnight to tell her about John's being in jail.

"John, dearest one, would they not release you, no matter how you begged for release?" Bitsy asked when she was allowed to enter the jail.

"No, Bitsy, there was no way out. I either had to promise I would not preach again, or else come to jail. You know, dear, that I could never promise that. How could I live with my conscience and disobey my God in this way?" John looked straight into her deep blue eyes. They looked tired.

"Oh, the wicked people of the government! Why do they have to have such ridiculous laws, John? Can they not see that this will bring the country to ruin? There can be no true freedom when men are not free to speak their minds about all things, especially religion."

"Let us have patience, my dear. We shall win in the end. There are many Pilgrims who have sailed for the new land of America, where there is complete freedom. Some have fled to the Continent. Many Baptists have gone to Holland and some have fled even from Ireland. But I do not wish to flee."

"Yes, I know, dearest. I will try not to worry any more than I can help.... I do hope the baby will be healthy and natural. We have both wanted this little one so much."

"Oh, yes, yes, I do pray the baby will be all right. Bitsy, dear, you simply must not worry about things just now. Let me do the worrying, seeing I don't have much else to do." John laughed softly.

"I do believe you'd laugh if you were waiting to be burned at the stake!" Bitsy said, patting his cheek. "Now I must go, John, dear. There is no one with the children except Mary. And she cannot mind them very well, though she does get around well with the new cane you made for her the other day. I will try to explain to them why you are here the best I can."

He kissed her, holding her close for a long moment. Then he released her. "You must go now, dearest one. Come back tomorrow, if you can."

The next day, when Bitsy came with food and fresh water, she brought a small bundle of laces which she had cut and made the day

82

before. "I asked Mr. Cobb this morning if you could help me with these, and he said you may. They need to be tagged in neat groups of twelve each—six pairs. He also said some of the prisoners sometimes sell things to passersby over the bridge on market days—Tuesdays and Saturdays. If you are not ashamed to try your hand at selling some, you could help us out this way," Bitsy said.

"Of course I'm not ashamed, not when its bread and butter to my dear family. After all, I am not here by any fault of my own."

For several weeks John tagged and sold the laces. Often people would come by and ask him for them, even on non-market days. They liked the extra-strong, good laces which Bitsy made.

For several days now Bitsy did not come to the jail.

✠  ✠  ✠

One morning early, John heard the shuffle of feet along the bridge. The door opened and in walked Paul Cobb, the chief jailer responsible for the prisoners. He hardly ever came to the jail, for Paul White, the deputy jailer, attended to the details of the prison. John wondered what was happening now, for he saw that Cobb wore a troubled expression.

"John, I have a bit of bad news for you. Your wife is very ill. The doctor has been there and says you should come to her, if you could; now, if you will promise me solemnly that you will not preach again nor hold any conventicles while you are out, I will allow you to go and see her and take your freedom for a few days." His eyes rested upon John.

John's heart was sick. Bitsy was ill, and possibly because she had been worrying far too much. They might even lose the baby they had both wanted so much. His thoughts raced to and fro. "What harm could there be in such a promise as this?" he wondered. But then he remembered, if he were seen outside the jail, people might wonder if he had compromised the Gospel for his own case.

"I love my wife and children very much, Cobb, and it hurts to be away from them, especially when Bitsy needs me so much just now. But rather than to conform to such promises, I will lie here until the moss grows over my eyes and lips, and my flesh falls from my bones."

"These men will not let a tinker stand in their way, John. You are acting foolishly."

A few minutes later, Paul White came into the jail. "I see ye been arguing with Cobb again, John. That don't pay. I was just thinking I believe ye are as tough as ye were in army days. Now I am surely sorry, but I have orders to lock ye in one of the dungeon rooms. It's pretty

83

damp and nasty and there are rats in there, too. I bemoan doing it, but I have no other way around it."

John's new cell was a small room back in the grain house, without windows or heat. There were several blankets, smelling musty and bad, on a narrow cot. One very small opening in the wall high in the room let in a little air.

When Bitsy heard from the children that John was in the dungeon room, it caused her to become violently ill again. Two days later, while John was still in the dungeon, Bitsy lost the baby. Dr. Banister came and delivered it and took care of her. He went by the jail and told Cobb what had happened and that John's wife was fretting herself to death. "Why did you place him in the dungeon, Cobb? What had he done to deserve this?" the doctor wanted to know.

"I offered him freedom to go and attend to his wife, if he would promise not to preach again while he was out, nor convene any conventicle," Cobb said churlishly.

"Cobb, you know Bunyan better than this. That is what he was imprisoned for in the first place—refusing to promise not to preach. A promise he would find it very difficult to keep. You are in authority here, I understand that fully, and you can do with the prisoners as you see fit, but you had no moral or legal right to put John into the dungeon. If you have not the morals of a scoundrel yourself, you will let him out of that dungeon right away!" the doctor said as he turned to go.

Cobb called Paul White and told him to release John from the dungeon the next morning, but to restrict his family's visiting rights to once every other day for a week.

✠ ✠ ✠

Christmas Day was not far away. John figured out as he lay on his straw mattress that this would be a skip day, on which his family would not be permitted to visit him. He could only hope and pray. On Christmas Eve, John sat in the small family room alone, wondering if his family would be able to come the next day. Christmas had always meant so much to them all.

John fell to daydreaming again when White was gone. For a moment or two, he even forgot the prison walls. Suddenly he had a strange impression. There appeared before his mind's eye, as if in a dream, a tall strong figure with a Pilgrim's staff in his hand. As he looked at this imagined character he spoke aloud to himself, "Christian, Christian! That shall be his name. I'll tell the children a story about Christian and his journey to the heavenly city, if they come tomorrow," he said aloud to himself. He began to think of a way to tell the story, and when he awoke from his reverie it was midnight. The fire had long since burned out and he was chilly from the cold air. Arising, he went to his bed and slept soundly and in great peace the rest of the night.

Early the next morning he awoke and dressed. He ate the poor gruel Paul brought to him almost in silence, except to ask, "Did you find out anything from Cobb about my family's coming today?"

"Yes, he said they may come. I notified your wife last night," Paul said as he left the jail.

"A Merry Christmas to you, Paul," John called after him.

"And you, too, good friend," Paul called back.

John drew out from under his bed some rough paper and a pen and ink. He made some notes of his newly developing story about "Christian" and his journey to the heavenly city.

Just before noon, the door opened and Bitsy and the children came into the jail. Paul let them in, telling them to stay as long as they wanted. The children ran to their father and hugged and kissed him. Thomas wanted to sit on his lap and John stood by his knee. Bitsy placed the heavy tray on a nearby stand which John had gotten from Paul for his writing, and came and kissed John.

All the children had brought something to him. John was very happy. Mary brought the little jug he had once brought home to her mother, filled with hot soup. "Hot soup, Papa," she said. "We decided to make this jug useful. I know Mama would want you to use it this way if she were here."

"Oh, thank you, thank you, sweet Mary girl," her father said. "You can bring me soup and milk in it from now on while I'm here—and I hope that will not be too long," he said, hugging Mary close to him as he sat on his three-legged stool.

Then they ate their Christmas dinner, amidst the chatter of the children's talk. "We have no want for anything, dear—except you," Bitsy smiled at him. "I do hope England will wake up to her sordid condition and change these awful laws which punish people for no greater crimes than doing good to others," she said.

When dinner was over and Bitsy had gathered the dishes into a large basket, the children gathered around John, asking him to tell them a story. "Tell us the best Christmas story you know, Papa," Mary said, as she pushed her fingers through his heavy shock of reddish-brown hair. It fell to his shoulders, where it curled upward slightly.

"Well, let me see, now. You have heard the Bible story about Christmas and the Savior's birth many times, so we will need to look for a new story. I have a new one which I have been thinking about. I hope you will like it," John started.

"What is it about, Papa, St. George and the dragon?" Mary wanted to know.

"No, it's a brand new story—one I have never told anyone before. It's about a man who started out on a journey to a very far away city. We shall call the man's name *Christian*, and the city he is going to we shall call the *Celestial City*." John remembered that Mary was blind and that much of the story she would not understand unless he was very descriptive in his story-telling.

"Christian was a very tall, strong man. He was about as old as your father and he wore the Pilgrim garments. He carried a staff in his hand, so he could find his way towards the heavenly city even when dark." John explained that the Pilgrim had not been a Christian at first. He described how burdened he was with his sins as he started out in search of the way. He told how Christian met Pliable and how they both fell into the Slough of Despond. Here Mary stopped him. "Papa, is the Slough of Despond the same as our slough used to be at Elstow?"

"I guess you might say something like that, Mary dear," he said, seeing that her ready mind had already caught the allegory of his story. He told how Evangelist showed the way to the Wicket Gate and how Christian lost his heavy burden of sin.

"That will be enough for this time, children. More later," John said. He did not tell them that this was as far as he had gotten with the story himself.

"Why do they keep you here, Papa?" John asked. He could not understand why his father did not come home.

"Because I preach the Gospel, telling people how to be saved and serve the Lord. I have no state license to preach."

"They don't put the vicar in jail for preaching, though, Papa," John observed.

"No, but he has a license and he preaches in the parish church. That is the church which the King and the government calls the true church," he explained.

"Oh, I must tell you," Bitsy put in. "Since you have been in jail, many have come to buy your books. Some are almost exhausted. You need to start writing some more. Maybe you could do some of this work in jail while waiting on the Sessions," Bitsy said.

"That's an excellent idea! Bring my unfinished manuscript and some ink when you come again. I only want the will of God for my life, Bitsy. Paul, the Apostle, did some of his most important work in prison. When my bail was refused by Chief Justice Compton, God sweetly met me here in the prison, comforting and satisfying me that it was His will that I should be here. Not one hair of my head can fall to the ground without the will of my Father who is in heaven. Let the rage and malice of men do what they will, they can go no farther and do no more than God permits. And even when they have done their worst, we can know that 'all things work together for good to them that love God.' Bitsy darling, we must be patient and wait."

Bitsy rose. "I must go, dearest one. The shadows are lengthening. I will come again as soon as I can, and I'll bring your writing materials. Maybe Mary can bring the manuscript when she comes tomorrow with your jug of soup."

✠  ✠  ✠

One evening a drummer stopped into the alehouse in Elstow. He was traveling from London to Glasgow and had stopped for the night. He seated himself at a table beside a large man and started talking. "What is this man John Bunyan like?" he asked. "I have heard about him all over the Midlands. He must have a powerful following. I heard he is in jail in Bedford."

"Yes, you have heard right. He used to live here till two or three years ago, when he moved to Bedford. He has a nice home there and a fine family. His first wife died and he married again, a lovely young woman who was educated at some girls' school, I understand." The speaker was Tad Simmons, John's boyhood friend.

"What's all the fuss about his being in jail, what did he do?"

"Nothing serious, just preached without a government license. His church in Bedford is a Meeters' Church, not a Parish Church, you see. He is not an ordained and recorded minister. More or less of a lay preacher, he is," Tad explained.

"Hats off to anyone willing to fight this government of Charles and Hyde ... mostly Hyde's, since the King spends his time with women and wine," the drummer said.

"I agree. I respect Bunyan. He and I grew up here together. I was in the Parliamentary Army with him at Newport. He was always serious, even before he took up the ministry."

"What's wrong with open-air preaching anyhow? It has a pretty lively history. There were the Franciscans and the preaching friars, and Wycliffe's men, dating back to the thirteenth and fourteenth centuries—long before these times," the drummer said.

"True, but this government is trying to force the Anglican Church on everyone. As a result, most of the people have none at all. The devil is surely turned loose today," Tad said.

"Tell me a bit about this Bunyan. What's he like? He has to have a strong appeal to raise all the furor I've been hearing about."

"Well, he's tall and strong, a tinker by trade. They call him the Tinker Preacher. His voice is clear and resonant and easy to listen to. He has a wonderful command of English and speaks fluently and freely. His years in the army and plying a trade have given him power with people. He uses tremendous illustrations and has a vivid imagination. His eyes are deep blue and shine out from beneath a high forehead like twinkling stars. He preaches with passion and power. Yet, he is a meek man, patient and self-disciplined. I'd say he's one of the best speakers in England," Tad said.

Tad noticed the man had been making notes while he talked. As he rose to go, the man said, "I'm only a part-time drummer. I'm really a reporter from the *Commonwealth Mercury* of London. This information will come in handy later when I do a report on Bunyan." The man stepped to the door and was gone. Tad did not get his name.

# chapter 10

The Bedford Quarter Sessions were slated for the second week in January 1661. The place of the meeting was the Herne Chapel, since Bedford had no regular courthouse. Herne Chapel was a gray stone building standing near the center of town. It was high and massive with just a few narrow windows. Behind the chapel were several common rooms. Even county fairs were sometimes held at Herne Chapel.

One morning, just before the Sessions opened, Paul Cobb came into the jail. "Just thought you'd like to know what judges will be presiding at the Sessions, John."

"Yes, that will be of interest. I hope we get a fair group of justices."

"Well I'm not so sure of that, not where you are concerned at least. Chief Justice Kelynge will be the main presiding officer," Paul said. "He hates Roundheads, you know, for they imprisoned him during the war for his Royalist sympathies. He'll find out you were in the Roundhead Army, never worry about that."

"What has that got to do with justice, Paul?"

"Nothing, of course, but you don't always get justice in these courts. Sometimes it's a matter of the whim of the judge."

"We can only hope for the mercy of the Lord," John said. "Who are the assisting judges this time?"

"Sir Henry Chester of Lidington, who's an uncle of Francis Wingate; George Blundell, who lost all he had under the Commonwealth Government. These two will certainly not be easy to get along with. Then there will also be Sir William Beecher of Howbury and Thomas Snaggy of Millbrook. These two will be more unprejudiced, if you could get one of them. But probably Kelynge will try your case."

"No doubt they intend to make an example of me," asserted Bunyan.

"You are a widely known man, John, as you know. Your writings have not helped matters. They are read all over England and the Continent. You are a thorn to them. Maybe that's why so many eminent judges are coming for the Sessions. We've never had so many before. I can only hope the Lord has mercy on ye, John."

John walked back and forth in the small jail room, facing the bridge. He poured out his soul in prayer to God for His guidance. When Bitsy came, he was more calm. "I'm so glad you came, Bitsy. I've been wanting to talk to you. Paul was just here and told me about the judges who will be here for the Sessions."

"Oh, John, don't be so melancholy, dear. God can do things which people cannot. He got Peter out of jail and He can get you out, too, if we trust Him enough. I'll be there with you, and others will do their best for you, as well. I am sure, dearest."

The next morning Paul Cobb came to take Bunyan to his trial. "John, I am sorry to tell you, but I heard this morning that Francis Wingate, William Foster, and William Vierney, your old schoolmaster, have been working against you. They would like to see you permanently jailed."

"I would naturally expect this of them all. Vierney never did like me, even when I was a boy in school."

"The recent uprising of the Fifth Monarchists in London will not be very helpful to your case, either, I fear. These crazy fellows maintain that Nebuchadnezzar, of the Babylonian empire; Darius, of the Persians; Alexander, of the Greeks; and Julius Caesar, of the Romans, all failed; and now, Jesus Christ, the Fifth Monarch, is going to set up His kingdom and destroy all others," Paul laughed. "How people can follow such ridiculous stuff is a riddle to me."

"But I have nothing to do with them, in any way, Paul. I have never been disloyal to the King or the government," stated Tinker John.

☩  ☩  ☩

They passed along the streets, and many cried out to Bunyan. Some said, "We are sorry to see ye suffer in this shameful way." Others said, "Our prayers be with you." Someone shouted, "Hello, Tinker. How is jail life? Hope ye get a good long term this time." Another called, "Good enough for ye, Roundhead simpleton."

A crowd stood outside the chapel. The building was already jammed. Just inside the door stood John's father, now stooped and graying, and his step-mother, Anne, with tears in her eyes. "God protect ye, son," she cried as she touched his sleeve as he passed.

"May God pity ye, son. You have rough judges—I fear they will not be very kind," Thomas Bunyan said, laying a hand on John's shoulder.

"Yes, I fear you are right, Papa," he said as he scanned the audience, looking for the most important face in the crowd.

Just then, Bitsy came up from behind him and slipped her arm through his. She squeezed his arm with her other hand. "I'm here, darling."

Presently, Chief Justice Kelynge pounded the desk and the court crier called out, "Hear ye, hear ye, come into court." Justice Kelynge was dressed in a long, flowing black robe. His hair was powdered and his wig properly in place. He was tall and rawboned, with a ruddy complexion and a high, massive forehead. He was a harsh, unrelenting man. He showed mercy only where circumstances forced him to do so.

Silence reigned. Every eye was fastened upon the judge. Kelynge lifted his hands, as if in a gesture to bless the people, and began his introduction. "The first case which we shall try is that of the prisoner, John Bunyan, against the nation of England, for preaching without a license, contrary to English law."

John cleared his throat. His heart sped up as he looked up into the face of Justice Kelynge. He tried to be composed. "Help me, Lord, not to deny Thee here today, but to speak only as becometh those who love and serve Thee," he prayed silently.

"The clerk will now read the charge against John Bunyan." Kelynge stared down at Bunyan with cold, hard eyes. John had been handed a bill of his indictment which he could read along with the clerk.

The clerk read in solemn tones:

John Bunyan, a local tinker of Bedford, who has dared to declare himself a minister and has proceeded to preach without a license, was indicted for devilishly and perniciously abstaining from coming to church to hear divine services and for being a common upholder of several meetings and conventicles to the great disturbance and distraction of the good subjects of this kingdom and contrary to the laws of our sovereign lord, the King.

The clerk relaxed and leaned back in his chair.

Chief Justice Kelynge shuffled the papers on his desk. "This sounds like a good case," he thought. "If we can make a good example of this country bumpkin and make him submit, maybe I will even be rewarded with a large office by the Lord Chancellor, Hyde."

Looking down at John with cold eyes, he commanded the clerk to question the prisoner.

"How do you plead, John Bunyan?" the clerk asked.

John, who had not employed an attorney, arose. "Your Honors, the Justices of this trial, I stand before you accused of refusing to come to church and of disturbing the peace by holding unlawful meetings. It is implied that I have committed treason. I have gone to God's Church and I am a member of a Christian body. I only wish to do good."

"Do you come to your parish church for service?" Kelynge asked sharply.

"No."

"Will you acknowledge the King's ecclesiastical supremacy."

"I acknowledge him as my King, but not as a king of my conscience."

The justices scowled at him in dismay. John remembered that only recently there had been an act passed forbidding "all unlawful and seditious meetings under the pretense of religion." But, John thought to himself, "I cannot acknowledge King Charles, the drunken adulterer, as ruler of my conscience. I will not condemn my soul by such profanity."

"Why do you not attend divine services?"

"God does not command my attendance at any one church."

"Doesn't He command you to pray?"

"Not from a particular Prayer Book," John replied.

"Then how?" the judge thundered at him.

"St. Paul said, 'I will pray with the spirit and with the understanding.'"

"Let him speak no more," roared Justice Chester. "He speaks like a common laborer."

Chief Justice Kelynge ignored his colleague. "The Book of Common Prayer has been in use since the days of the Apostles," he said. Several people in the court room snickered at this ignorant remark.

"Your Honor, sir," said John, "would you please show me a verse in the New Testament which commands me to use it?" Several people in the chapel laughed softly. Kelynge's face flushed with red, as he realized his blunder.

"You need to pray!" he shouted.

"I can pray very well without it," John said.

Justice Blundell came to Kelynge's rescue with sharp words. "Then Beelzebub is your God," he cried in fury at John.

"If so, it is odd that we have the comforting presence of God among us at our meetings. Blessed be His holy name!" John replied.

"Peddler's French," Kelynge snorted. "Leave off your canting. What makes you, a mere tinker, think you are called of God to preach to men?"

"'As every man hath received the gift, even so let him minister the same unto another, as good stewards of the manifold grace of God.' St. Peter said this. I am only following these directions. What harm is there in this?"

"Then follow your gift of tinkering and let the educated preachers follow their calling to preach," Kelynge shouted at him. His face was red, and he was plainly agitated at John's boldness. He had not broken him down as he had so hoped to do, nor had he really trapped him in any of his statements.

The Chief Justice continued, "Then you confess the indictment. Your long chatter for a plea is tantamount to being guilty by confession, by standard procedures of the courts."

John squared his shoulders and stood tall and erect. There was a calm and benign look upon his face. He looked straight into the cold eyes of Kelynge and said solemnly, "I confess we have meetings to exhort one another. *I do not confess any guilt!*"

Kelynge was disturbed. He cleared his throat and said, "Let the accused hear the sentence of this court. You are to be held in jail three months longer. If you refuse to attend your parish church, you will be banished from England. Should you return without special permission from the King, your neck will be stretched."

A murmur ran through the courtroom. Many people were shocked and shook their heads in disbelief. Spontaneously, they arose and came forward, many expressing sympathy to John.

One large fellow with tears streaming down his cheeks declared, "We believe in you as we always did, no matter what these wicked judges have done to you."

Many of the women hugged Bitsy and promised to stand by her. The justice, seeing this show of affection and sympathy, realized he had really lost his case. But he had made a public example for the King of such fellows as may defy his laws.

As the bailiffs took John by the arm to lead him out, he turned and shouted up at the justices, "If I were out of jail today, I would preach the Gospel tomorrow!"

Kelynge said to his colleagues, "I have no doubt of that. I never saw a more stubborn, determined man. I hate him, yet in a way I admire him, too. He has the courage of a lion."

# chapter 11

The January wind blew through the cracks in the old city jail, to which John had been taken. Paul Cobb had been by and talked with John. Things were in a ferment in London, where some were pressing for another Toleration Act. There was little hope it would do John Bunyan any good.

The last days of January were slipping by swiftly. John had done little work on his book of late. He had been tagging and selling laces, mostly, to help support his family. Mary had been bringing him his jug of soup and other things almost daily.

John sat thinking. Bitsy had come in the morning after his trial. She had said, "John, my darling, we know one thing this morning—you have more friends that really care about you than we ever dreamed you had, or at least than I ever thought."

"Yes, Bitsy dear, we surely do have friends, and that is good," John had replied, "but that doesn't set me free nor give you and the children bread and clothes. I am worried about you oftentimes. And my poor dear blind Mary. My heart aches for her. She seems to love me so desperately. I wonder what will become of her in this world."

"John, you speak as if you will *never* get out of this old jail. Don't talk this way, dear. Surely, there'll be a way out. It cannot be this bad that you will *never* get out. I know what I am going to do. I am going to London to see the King himself or some of his ministers and plead your case myself. Mr. Harrington says it may do some good."

"That would be far too risky a trip for my darling to take, just for me, and then most likely it would only be for naught," John said.

"But I can certainly try," Bitsy had said as she rose to leave.

February passed with little of note occurring, except that John Rusk, the famous Quaker who had fought for religious freedom, was placed in jail with John. They discussed many things about the Quakers and their doctrines, and John came to understand them much better. Rusk had brought with him Foxe's *Book of Martyrs*. It was a great solace to his own soul to see how others had suffered for Christ across the ages. They had established regular weekly services for the prisoners, and John had preached several times. "They can't even put me in jail for this," he remarked to a fellow prisoner one day, with a twinkle in his eye.

"Why not?" the prisoner asked.

"They can't put a man in jail who is already there," Bunyan said calmly.

It was now early March, and John knew that any day Bitsy would set out on her London trip. He had been working on a new book, *Praying in the Spirit*, which he hoped to have ready for the printers by the spring. John thought how fast time had flown by as he realized that it was already the spring of 1661.

One morning, late in March, Bitsy came to the jail dressed in a beautiful green dress with a Pilgrim collar and hat. She carried a large purse.

"And whither now is my sweet lady planning to go? Surely not just to the jail, looking so trim as all this?" John's eyes sparkled with delight as he beheld her. He knew her answer.

"To London, of course. I'm leaving on the morning coach," Bitsy said. "The Bedford Meeting people have given me the money and are caring for the children. Mary will bring your meals. You must not worry about a thing, now, dear. Do pray for the success of my mission. Mr. Harrington thinks I should try to see Chancellor Hyde."

"You are a noble ambassador, Mrs. Bunyan," John said teasingly. "I do hope you have a safe passage and that you will accomplish your desire." John watched her until she disappeared in the crowd at the end of the bridge.

Elizabeth Bunyan had been recommended to the home of a Puritan minister in London. Although she was but a poor girl from Bedfordshire, her early schooling had given her a graceful way and the knowledge of how to manage in polite society.

At first she failed to gain admittance to Chancellor Hyde's offices. "The Chancellor is far too busy to waste time with a country woman who is interested in only some trivial affair," the guard said briskly.

"Hear me, sir," Elizabeth said to the guard. "I come not for myself nor even for my family alone. I have a concern that is of importance to the whole British domain. I demand to see the Chancellor."

"All right, all right lady. I'll show you into his outer offices. It will be up to his secretary whether or not you see him."

Elizabeth was awed by the huge building, with its many pictures and expensive tapestries. She was about to knock on the massive door for admission when it opened and out stepped Chancellor Hyde.

"Are you Chancellor Hyde, sir?"

"I am, lady. Did you not see a secretary here?"

"There was none at the desk, sir, so I had intended to knock on the door; just then you came out," Elizabeth said quietly.

Hyde looked at her. Her dress suggested a Puritan but her hairstyle and deportment belied it. The Chancellor could not make up his mind about her.

"I am Elizabeth Bunyan, the wife of John Bunyan, of Bedford. I have come to see you about my husband, but also about much more than just his interests—the interests of many hundreds who suffer imprisonment as he does today." Chancellor Hyde was taken by surprise.

"Come into my office, lady, if you will, please, and I shall speak to you of this matter," he said, turning back. When she was seated in his office the Chancellor said, "Now, what is it you are here to petition me for, about religious prisoners, did you say?"

"That is right, sir. My husband has been in jail now for many months. We have neither food nor clothes, except what the good people of the parish give to us."

"And why is he there?"

"For preaching the Gospel without a license. He is a duly accredited and ordained minister in the Bedford Meeting of the Meeters. He has done no one any harm, sir, and for so small a thing as conducting a meeting in a farmhouse last November he has been imprisoned without release. When the Quarter Sessions were held in January they had a mock trial for him and returned him to jail to await the Summer Sessions. There are hundreds more like him all over the country who are suffering similarly for no greater crimes than his. I am here to plead with you, sir, to ask the King for an Act of Toleration that these innocent people may go free." Elizabeth sat motionless, looking straight at the Chancellor.

"The Chancellor does not make the laws of the land," Hyde said.

"I know that, sir. But you most certainly have the power to petition the King."

Hyde ignored her reference to his petitioning the King. "Mrs. Bunyan, I cannot help you. I am sorry. Tell your husband to appeal to the judges in his area. It's up to them, not me." Hyde rose as a signal she should go, but Elizabeth did not rise. "Sir, I do not represent John Bunyan alone, but most of the people of Bedfordshire, as well as hundreds of other prisoners. I wish to know whether you will petition the King for an Act of Toleration. I have a duty to my people and the people of the shire."

"Possibly it would do no good if I did petition the King. Charles has a mind of his own," asserted Hyde.

"But sir, you are the Chancellor of *all* the people of this kingdom, not merely of those who agree with your beliefs. There should be freedom for men to worship God according to their consciences. There will never be real peace in this realm until this comes about."

"You are an unusual woman," he said. "I admire you. I will speak to the King about an Act of Toleration, but these things do not happen overnight. My advice is that you go back to Bedford and see if you can contact Sir Matthew Hale when the Summer Sessions are held. He is a kindly person and may be able to help you."

Thanking the Chancellor, Elizabeth arose and left. Back at the Puritan minister's residence, they could hardly believe her story. "You have done better with Hyde than anyone has in a long time," laughed the vicar. "We can only hope he will carry through his promise and that the Act will be granted, but as he said, this will require time."

✠ ✠ ✠

Back at the jail, John sat in silent meditation, quill in hand, placing the finishing touches on his manuscript, *Praying in the Spirit*. April the first had dawned clear and beautiful. John was wishing he could go for a walk in the woods.

Just then the jail door opened and in stepped Bitsy. Her face was radiant. She ran into John's arms. "I returned late last night from London, darling, and from seeing Chancellor Hyde. I think I have some good news for you," she said breathlessly.

"Don't build up any false hopes, now, dearest one."

"But I asked Hyde to make a petition to the King for an Act of Toleration, so that not only you but all religious prisoners could be set free," Bitsy beamed.

"And what was his answer to that? I don't expect you got far on that score, did you?"

"After I told him I was there to represent not only you, but all others who are imprisoned like you, that I represented the shire, the Bedford Meeting and many other people, he was very thoughtful for awhile. Then he said he admired me. But the best thing is, he actually promised to speak to the King. Isn't that good, John?"

"You are a brave girl," John smiled. "But don't get your hopes too high. We will not likely see any results from such an act for quite a long time."

"No, he said we would have to get the petition before the King, and this would require time," Bitsy said. "But he did encourage me to see judge Sir Matthew Hale this summer when he comes to Bedford for the Sessions. He thought maybe Sir Hale could help us.

"I certainly do hope so. I have about finished this new book, so you can take this and recopy it for me, Bitsy girl. I'll start work on another one while we wait." John smiled broadly at Bitsy. "Many thanks for the long hard journey to London and all you did there for me and the others. It may yet pay off."

✠ ✠ ✠

Later in the spring, the Quaker prisoner, Rusk, fell ill and died in the prison. John was greatly saddened at his passing. After the man had been buried, John fell into a state of depression. When Bitsy came in the morning after Rusk's burial, John greeted her in a depressed state of mind. "Bitsy, I am deeply melancholy and I cannot seem to throw it off. My being parted from you and my dear children and being in this place often becomes unbearable."

"But we must keep faith, John, dear, for God will work in some strange way for your deliverance."

"It is easier for you to say that outside of this terrible place than it would be if you were in here. Oh, my poor blind Mary—I love her more than all else in life, I suppose. Oh, the thought of the hardships my blind one may yet undergo breaks my heart." John placed his head on Bitsy's shoulder and sobbed deeply, his whole frame shaking. She patted his head, running her fingers through his hair.

"You must not worry so, dear one. God does know all, and it is for His cause that you are here. You have tagged hundreds of bundles of laces and sold them and provided income for us. Cheer up now, and be strong. 'The Lord will not fail thee nor forsake thee.'"

✝ ✝ ✝

Spring glided into summer while John worked on another book. Bitsy reworked *Praying in the Spirit*, getting it ready for the printer. John worked on more laces, selling a large quantity that spring. The Quarter Sessions would soon be in town again and Bitsy determined to see Sir Matthew Hale and try to get John released.

Discovering that Sir Matthew was in the vicinity, she borrowed a horse and rode to Harrowden where he was staying. When he was introduced, she said simply, "Your Honor, sir, I am Elizabeth Bunyan, wife of John Bunyan, now held in prison for preaching in the shire. He is in Bedford jail and I have come to implore you to please release him."

"Why is he imprisoned for preaching, madam?" Sir Matthew asked.

"Because, sir, he has no license, but he feels that God has called him to preach, and therefore, he must do it. He was imprisoned by Justice Wingate last fall, after being caught conducting a Gospel service near Harlington," she explained.

"Was he not tried at the January Quarter Sessions?"

"Yes, Your Honor, after a fashion, he was tried. But he did not plead guilty. He had not been preaching when they apprehended him, only opening a service with prayer and the reading of the Bible," Elizabeth explained. "I come to you, sir, because Chancellor Hyde recommended that I see you."

Sir Matthew arched his eyebrows. "So you have contacted the Chancellor about this, have you?"

"Yes, early this spring. I also asked him to speak to the King about an Act of Toleration for all religious prisoners," Elizabeth said.

"Very well. I will look into your husband's case and do what I can," Sir Matthew promised Bitsy.

The following day, Judge Twisden was passing through St. Paul's Square in Bedford in his coach. Elizabeth ventured to toss a note into the open window of the coach to him, imploring him to have mercy on her husband and release him. Elizabeth knew that Twisden was to sit in the court as one of the judges with Sir Matthew. Looking at the note, Twisden flew into a rage and stormed after her—"It is of no use for you to be handing notes to me; your husband cannot be released until he promises not to preach any more!" he shouted angrily as the coach went on.

Undaunted, Elizabeth went into the courtroom the next day and waited for an opportunity to speak to Sir Matthew Hale again. Elizabeth thought Sir Matthew was an honorable man and somewhat religious. He had shown her courtesy. She whispered a prayer for help and approached his bench, asking to speak to him.

"Yes, madam, what is it that you wish to speak to me about?"

"I think you know, good sir; it is about my husband, John Bunyan, who has been unjustly imprisoned for no greater crime than preaching the Gospel of Christ," Elizabeth said.

The haughty Sir Henry Chester, sharing the bench with Sir Matthew that day, interrupted her immediately. "Sir Matthew, her husband has been duly convicted of preaching against the laws of the kingdom. He is a hot-spirited Gospeller, and you can expect nothing more from him than that he will stir up more trouble; he will not leave off preaching."

"I am very sorry, young woman, but there is nothing further I can do for you. I have looked into the matter since we talked, and it seems I cannot do anything for your husband," Sir Matthew said. He looked at Elizabeth with fatherly pity.

Great tears welled up in Elizabeth's large blue eyes. She looked for a long moment at Sir Matthew and then walked slowly away.

Later in the day, court adjourned. Elizabeth stayed near the chapel all the rest of the day, despite her rejection by Sir Matthew that morning. She prayed for the strength to go to the judge again. "As Esther of old, I shall go in and present my case again; and if I perish, I can but perish, but I shall have done my best for my dear husband."

Opening the door to the chamber cautiously, Elizabeth entered. Pressing her way through the crowd, she came straight forward to where Sir Matthew Hale was sitting. With a trembling heart Elizabeth said to him, "My Lord, I make bold to come once again to Your Lordship. I plead earnestly that you will grant mercy to my good husband, John Bunyan, who is unjustly imprisoned. He has never been lawfully convicted of any crime, and indeed, he has never even answered to the indictment against him," she said.

At this, Judge Twisden became angry and stormed at her, "Woman, I told you we can do nothing for this fellow!"

Judge Chester was even more bitter, storming at her angrily, "I tell you woman, this man is *convicted*, I care not what you say. It is recorded—*it is recorded*—in the records! Now, be gone and trouble us no further."

Undaunted even at this, Elizabeth turned to Sir Matthew with beseeching eyes and said, "Please, Your Lordship, let me speak a word to you of this matter." Sir Matthew nodded agreeably and Elizabeth went on. "Sometime ago, I went to London myself, and you know what a hard journey this is for a poor, common woman. I delivered my petition to Chancellor Hyde. He showed my petition to members of the House of Lords. They told him they would commit my husband's release to the judge at the next assize.[†] I had hoped that this would have been given to you. Sir Matthew, my husband is a good man—one who loves his Lord and honors his King and his country," she pleaded.

At this, Judge Chester, true to his character, flew into a rage and shouted at Elizabeth scornfully, "How many more times do I have to tell you, woman, that your husband stands *convicted*! That is a matter of *record*!" Turning to the other judges he said, "This Bunyan is a pestilent fellow, stirring up the countryside with his unlawful preaching. There is not a fellow like him in the country. He gathers the crowds and excites them with his raging preachments."

Judge Twisden interposed, "Will your husband leave off his preaching if he be released?"

"My Lord," replied Elizabeth, "he cannot leave off preaching. Can you not understand that God has called him to proclaim His Word? What harm can come to the realm from this?"

"What more use is there talking about this matter, if he will not leave off preaching?" Twisden asked. "He would be right back in prison again for the same offense."

"But there is need for his release, my Lord," Elizabeth replied. "I have four small children that cannot help themselves. One of them is blind, and we have nothing to live upon but the charity of good people," she pleaded.

Sir Matthew Hale was moved. He touched her hand lightly and exclaimed, "Alas, poor woman! I am sorry, but I have seen no papers of petition for him. Someone must have failed to pass them on to me."

When Twisden saw that Hale was beginning to soften up a bit, he became very angry. "Get out of this chamber, woman," he yelled at her. "You make poverty a mere cloak for trying to get your wishes. Your hus-

---

† In England, an *assize* is a trial session, civil or criminal, that is held intermittently by a high court.

band finds it a better thing to run up and down the country, preaching, than to follow his calling."

"What is his calling?" asked Sir Matthew.

"A tinker, my Lord," shouted a chorus of voices from the room.

"Yes," said Elizabeth, dauntless in her courage, "he is, and because he is a poor man, therefore he is despised and cannot have justice!"

Sir Matthew touched her arm. "I recommend that you either apply to the King directly, or sue out your husband's pardon, or try to obtain a writ of error in trial. I am sorry, my dear girl, that I can do no more for you, for you certainly are a dauntless lady."

This advice meant little to Elizabeth, who did not understand such matters. With this, she turned to leave the chamber. Judge Chester, still very angry, muttered to Hale, "My Lord, he will preach and do what he likes no matter what you do to help him."

To which Elizabeth, now quite upset, replied, "He preaches nothing but the Word of God!"

At this, Twisden, white with rage shouted, "*He* preach the Word of God!" He raised his open hand as if he would strike her, exclaiming, "He runneth up and down the country and doth harm to many people!"

Standing firmly, Elizabeth looked at him with tender eyes and replied, "No, my Lord, it is not so; God has owned him and done much good by him."

"God?" exclaimed the angry man, his face convulsing with rage. "His doctrine is the doctrine of the devil!"

Elizabeth stood with quiet dignity. "My Lord, when the Righteous Judge shall appear, it will be known that his doctrine is not the doctrine of the devil!" A hush came over the court; Elizabeth had the stage to herself.

She looked squarely at the judges. "I weep not for myself, nor for John Bunyan; our case is in God's hands. I weep to think of what a sad day it will be when you poor creatures who have so treated him today shall stand before the Judge of the universe to give an account of your deeds!" And turning, she walked out of the Swan Chambers, a woman of the most heroic courage.

✠ ✠ ✠

At the prison, John received her with his customary smile and gentle embrace.

"How went things for us today, my darling?" he said as he set the food down on a nearby stool and took the jug from her hand to take a drink of the fresh water.

"Dearest, I did my best. I made a plea for you far beyond what I could have believed myself able to do this morning. Your friend, Mr. Morton, was there and he can tell you how it went," Elizabeth said.

Not giving her time to finish, John said, "Did they hear your plea, and will they grant my release?"

"Sir Matthew was very courteous and listened with patience to my plea, but Chester and Twisden fought it to the finish and said many angry things to me. Twisden even raised his hand and I believe he would have struck me had he dared. He was white with rage," she said.

"So we lost the pleas," Bunyan said.

"Yes, darling, we lost today in this earthly court," she said, laying her head gently upon his shoulder. "But we shall win later in the heavenly court."

"It breaks my heart to be separated from you and the sweet children," said John. "I could go free tomorrow, I suppose, would I renounce all preaching and surrender my conscience to the present scheme of things." He drew a deep breath and straightened up his shoulders. "But Bitsy, darling, then I would have to betray my Lord and Savior and forsake His good Kingdom. I would fall back into the despond of former years and my guilt would become unbearable. I think I would go mad if I did this. *No!* Ten thousand times, *No!* I will *not* forsake my Lord, nor fail to declare His Holy Word upon every opportunity, even if it means imprisonment for life!"

# chapter 12

When Paul White came into the jail that evening, he said to John, "I have a bit of good news for you."

"Not a parole or anything like that, is it?" John said.

"No, hardly that good, John, but still much better than this. You are to be transferred to the county jail on Lane Street. That's much closer to your home, and it is also far better than this hole."

John lay for a long time that night before falling asleep, thinking what the county jail would be like. It was still a prison, of course, but there were many more prisoners and more conveniences there. He would have a greater opportunity to preach Christ to the inmates of the county jail.

Three days later, John was moved to the county jail. It was a large stone building in the center of the city on Lane Street. It had two stories, with a basement where there were dark dungeons for the worst prisoners, a main floor where the lesser offenders were kept, and a second floor for short term prisoners. The rooms were bigger and had eight-foot ceilings. Facing the street was a large common room with a fireplace where the prisoners could gather for conversation or to do work of various kinds. John's room was on the side of the wall and had a high window which let in sufficient light for reading and writing. It was drier and the beds were better, although the prisoner's relatives still had to provide most of the bedding.

The morning after John's transfer, Bitsy came to see him and brought the children. She wanted them to see where their father was now staying and to teach Mary how to find the building when she came alone. John showed them about the place.

"Oh, John, this is almost a palace compared to the old jail on the bridge!" Bitsy exclaimed when they had completed the tour of the building. John had his own room but was not confined to it. He was free to roam over the entire building and talk with the prisoners or do whatever he wanted.

"How fast the children are growing up, Bitsy. I'm sorry I cannot be with you to help with them. But when they are naughty, bring them to me, and I'll help you take care of them."

"Does that mean we get to go to jail, too, Papa?" Elizabeth asked.

John held her tightly, realizing how much she felt the need of her father. Smiling down at her, he replied, "Well, not exactly. It may mean that if you do not obey Mama Bitsy, you will have to be brought over here for me to spank occasionally."

"Oh, then I'll be naughty sometimes, so I can come and see you," she replied.

"So will I," blared John.

"I can come to bring you soup and food almost every day here, Papa," Mary chimed in. "It's not far and I will know the way soon. With my stick I can find the way, I'm sure."

John kissed her. She stroked his hair and placed her arms about his shoulders. "How big you are growing, Mary girl," he exclaimed. "You are now eleven years old and will soon be a young woman." Mary was tall for her age, with dark brown curls hanging about her slender shoulders. She was a delicate child and had never been very strong. She was intelligent and had memorized much of the Bible by that time.

That night, after the family had left and the other prisoners had gone to bed, John sat for a long time staring into the starry heavens from the window in the family room. "I might as well prepare myself for a long imprisonment," he reflected. "If I prepare for only a short term, I shall be sure to get a longer one, and only be disappointed in the end. I may as well even expect the worst—the whip and the pillory, or even banishment."

The next morning when Bitsy came, John was radiant. "Did you sleep well, dear? Is this a better place to think and meditate with all the rest of the prisoners around than the old jail on the bridge?" Bitsy wanted to know.

"Last night I had a strong battle with the enemy of my soul. He tried to plague me until past the midnight hour, but I got the victory over him."

"Yes, thank God, John, for grace to overcome," Bitsy whispered.

"I would not be without the experience of last night for anything. I am comforted when I think of it. I shall bless God forever for what I learned from it," John said.

A few days later, Paul White, who was the deputy jailer for the county jail as well as the city jail, came into John's room. "Is there anything I can get for you, John, to help make ye a bit more comfortable?" he asked.

"One thing, Paul, if you can get it—a good writing table. I need it for my work you know."

"You shall have it. I know where there is a fine one, and I'll bring it in right away." Paul was gone a few minutes and returned with a good, substantial table which John had him place in the large common room, since there was more light there than in his own. Everyone in the jail knew of Bunyan's writing. The table became known among the prisoners as "Bunyan's writing table."

✛ ✛ ✛

The months came and went now even faster than before. There were many Dissenters and Quakers in the jail from time to time, most of whom were in deep sympathy with Bunyan. There were debtors, too, in there because they could not pay their debts.

On Sundays, Bunyan was generally the jail's preacher. At times others among the Dissenters and Quakers also preached the Word. The prisoners as a whole attended these services, and sometimes outsiders came in for the meetings. Bitsy often brought the children when she knew that John would be preaching.

Among notable prisoners there were Samuel and John Fenne, who were members of the same church as Bunyan. They were thrown into prison for preaching at conventicles. William Wheeler, Rector at Cranfield, was turned out of his living and forbidden to preach when the King returned. He had dared to preach to a congregation of believers and was caught by officers of the law and placed there with others who had committed similar offenses. Many who were released from prison went out to lead Christian lives which would bless others. Often these converts would return to the prison to relate their happy experiences in witnessing to others of the power of Christ to save from sin.

Among the many listeners, after Bunyan was transferred to the county jail, was Paul White. Paul never seemed to pay much attention to the few services conducted in the old city jail, but the much larger ones in the county jail attracted him. He would stand outside the common room where the services were conducted and listen.

After several weeks, John noticed a change in Paul. He stopped swearing and became much more kind and understanding with the prisoners. He often took extra time with them and did whatever he could to make them comfortable. His callused nature changed, and he became kind and thoughtful. One day, when John was alone in the common room, Paul came into the room and seated himself on a chair. "John, I want to talk with you a little this morning about the matter of my soul's salvation."

"Yes, Paul, I will be delighted to talk with you."

"Well, I have been listening carefully to your sermons. God has convicted me of sin and I have repented and sought forgiveness. I praise God that He has forgiven my sins and redeemed me. Now, I want to be baptized," Paul said, his face radiant with joy.

"God be thanked, Paul, that you have turned from the darkness of sin to the light of Christ! I rejoice to know that God has brought you to Himself in this manner. And you can surely be baptized. We can arrange for this," stated the tinker turned preacher.

"What mode of baptism should it be?"

"That must be your decision, Paul. As you know, at the Bedford Meeting we baptize according to the wishes of the person."

"I thought if I were sprinkled, then ye could do it for me, since you cannot go out to baptize me in a stream anywhere, and there be no way of immersion here in the jail."

"Well, Paul, I guess we can do it here as St. Paul did long ago, when he baptized the jailer. I can sprinkle you in a Sunday morning service when you are ready."

The following Sunday morning, Paul was baptized by John in the jail and there was much rejoicing among the believers as he accepted the baptismal vows. Later, Pastor Burton took Paul into the Bedford Meeting.

During the fall months, John continued to write and preach and to counsel with many of the prisoners about the things of God. Sometimes when the children came on Sunday afternoons he would tell them more of the story of Christian and his journey to the Celestial City. He kept working out a set of characters as he slowly wove for them the story of Pilgrim.

John had also been working on the new book, *The Holy City*, during the fall days. Bitsy took parts of it to copy and kept it at the house, as there was less chance of it getting misplaced there. *Praying in the Spirit* had gone to the printers and was awaiting release. Bunyan's books were now reaching a wide audience and were beginning to stir much comment among the people. Although he himself was locked in Bedford jail, his writings had begun to go abroad in England and move people to thinking.

One day, a Quaker was brought into the jail for preaching without a license. He had often been in the London area. Over the years, John had changed his opinion of the Quakers. Laying his hand lightly upon the Quaker's shoulder, John said, "I thank God that He has given me a better understanding about the Quakers, although I do not yet fully understand nor agree with everything they teach."

"Nor do I agree with all of them, for some have gone astray from the original teachings of George Fox. They have become fanatics, saying they need not the Bible as their guide, since they have the Inner Light of the Holy Spirit abiding in them. George Fox never taught this. It is an extreme some have developed who follow false teachers. But many are seeking the light and turning from this evil teaching," the Quaker told John.

☩ ☩ ☩

It was Christmas Eve again now. John sat before the large open fireplace musing on his story of Christian which he would tell the children the next day. As he thought about it he scribbled down a few notes. The jail door opened quietly and in stepped Paul Cobb. John turned in surprise at seeing him there at that time. "Anything wrong, Paul?" he asked.

"No, not at all," Paul almost whispered. "Not so loud, John, lest ye wake up the others. I've come to do ye a favor tonight. Ye can go home for the night, if ye will promise to come back before daylight in the morning, so no one will see ye," Paul said, smiling.

"Are you sure it will be all right, Paul? I don't want to make trouble for you."

"It will be all right, John; the William Fosters are gone to London for Christmas and there are no other troublemakers around here now. Just don't tell the others. I can't let them all out, ye know," Paul assured him.

John slipped into his best clothes and hurried out the door while Paul waited for him. Paul then gave him the key to the huge door, so he could open it when he returned in the morning. As John walked along the dark alley from Lane Street leading toward St. Cuthbert's Parish and his home, his mind raced with all sorts of imaginations as to what Bitsy and the children would think of his being out of prison for the night. Just as he rounded the corner near St. Cuthbert's Church the town crier announced, "Ten o'clock and all's well ... Christmas will soon be here ... Have a merry one everybody!"

John thought, "A merry one indeed it will be for me."

When he came to the door and knocked, he heard the children squeal. He knew they had not gone to bed. Bitsy came to the door, her hands wet with dishwater. She had been washing the pots and pans from her Christmas dinner cooking. "Oh, John, how did you get here?" she said in a low voice, remembering not to alarm the neighbors. "Come in, you darling. We were all just planning and fixing things for you tomorrow," she said as he swept her into his arms and kissed her. After a long moment, he let her down and then Elizabeth rushed into his arms. Mary stood patiently waiting her turn, until the rest of the children had greeted him.

"Will you spend Christmas day with us, Papa? We have lots of hickory nuts from the woods and Mama Bitsy has made a big pudding, and Mary has made you some things," Thomas said, glancing over at Mary. He had almost told what Mary had made for him before he thought. Mary, who had bitten her lip, now relaxed a bit.

"No, children, I am only allowed to come home for the night. I must go back before daybreak in the morning, so no one will know I am out. Paul Cobb was very good to allow me to come home even for the night," he explained.

Mary now came to her father and placed her arms about his neck and sat down on his lap by the large open fire in the family room.

"I have memorized all the story you have told us about Christian so far, Papa," Mary said as she stroked his hair with her hand. "Will you tell us more about him tomorrow? May we come to the jail and see you and hear more about Christian in the afternoon, as we did last year?"

"Yes, my dearest angel, you surely may. I was just working on more of the story when Paul Cobb came in tonight to allow me to come home."

A few minutes later, the children were playing a game. Thomas asked his father to join them. "I have almost forgotten the time I have been away," he said as he sat down before the fire to join in.

"Oh, John, I had good news for you tomorrow, but I may as well tell you now. There was a letter for us in the mail today from your publisher at London. *Praying in the Spirit* is to be issued in January. The license has been secured and the printer will issue five thousand for the first run," Bitsy told him.

John's heart skipped a beat. "Wonderful news," he said joyfully as he followed her into the kitchen. There was a huge Christmas pudding cooling on the sideboard. The ducks were slowly baking in the oven and the kitchen smelled so good John could hardly stand to be in there without eating something.

"Here, dearest, since you cannot be here for Christmas dinner, you must have some pudding now," Bitsy said as she gave him a dish.

"John, dear, I have another surprise for you. In the letter from the printer was a check for the books he has sold during the past year. We will now have money for many of the things which we need this winter," Bitsy said as John finished his pudding.

"Fifty pounds!" John exclaimed holding up the check. "This will help us through the winter and even the whole year. The books must be selling very well."

"See, dear, you are helping us far more than you thought. Your writing is beginning to pay off," Bitsy said, patting him on the shoulder.

Since John could not remain for the next day, the family gathered about the large fireplace and sang Christmas carols and played games until well into the night. It was a most happy evening. John told the children the story of the Christ child, and about the wise men, and the trip to Egypt. After he had finished Mary spoke up, "Papa, it seems that ever since Jesus was born there has been persecution about Him. Even as a tiny Babe, they had to go to Egypt for fear of the king. Now, you are in prison because you have told others about Jesus. Will it ever be any different?"

"My dear sweet child," John said, drawing her to him, "we surely hope that some day all men will be able to worship God as freely as they feel they should. This is one reason I am in prison. I hope by staying there and writing to show other men the way of true freedom, so that some day all men will be free to go to the church they wish, or preach wherever they wish. It is even possible the laws can be changed so that everyone will be protected, whether Anglican, Catholic, Dissenter, or Quaker. This is my hope and prayer, and this is why I am willing to stay in prison for the present time."

Mary was very still for a moment, then she spoke. "Papa, it may be that in many years from now thousands of people will remember the great work you did in prison that others may be free."

At five o'clock John heard the town crier announce the hour. He knew he must arise and go. Bitsy was sound asleep when he left. As he neared the prison, he looked up at the twinkling stars and thought of the first Christmas morning, long ago. John turned the key in the lock, opened the great double door and easily slipped inside, locking the door behind him. The door made a slight squeak when it opened. John caught his breath and hoped the prisoners had not heard it. He slipped off his shoes and tiptoed to his bedroom where he went to bed.

✙ ✙ ✙

The children had their Christmas dinner with Bitsy at home. Just past noon, Bitsy and the children were let into the jail by Paul White. They brought gifts and a hot Christmas dinner for John. Since there were other visitors in the common room, John's family went into his room.

After he had eaten, John went on with his story about Christian and his journey to the Celestial City. He had just passed Christian through the Wicket Gate. Now, Christian went to Vanity Fair where he met Mr. Worldly-Wise-Man. Here poor Christian ran into more trouble. It was not long after this that he also was brought before Judge Hate-Good. When John told this part of the story, Mary cried out, "Oh, I know who he is. He's Judge Kelynge, that mean man who sentenced you to prison, Papa, that's who he is!"

John winked at Bitsy. He was amused that Mary had guessed right. John said, "You could be right, Mary. We all make our places in real life pretty much. Why not in a story?"

The children then clapped their hands. "That's a good story, Papa; it gets better and better," John said. "Will you write it in a book sometime for other children to read?" John had just entered the village school and was beginning to appreciate reading. Bitsy had taught him the alphabet and gotten him into reading well before he started to school.

"Now, that's an idea. I just might do that someday when we get the story finished."

Bitsy, who had been quietly listening, spoke up. "John, dear, if you could put this story into writing, in time it might become your greatest book. People have always loved stories. Jesus was a great storyteller, and your most effective sermons are those illustrated by your stories."

"I don't know, Bitsy; People are funny about religious things. I fear this would sound like some fairy story, or something unreal, and they would not accept it."

"There's only one sure way to find out—try it!" Bitsy said.

# chapter 13

The winter months dragged slowly along for the prisoners in Bedford Jail, but John was busy most of the time. He prepared sermons for the services and made ample notes for his books, some of which he would not write for some time to come. But as he thought of good ideas, he put them down. He also spent much time comforting those who had recently been brought into the prison, or who had lately been saved. His counseling ministry grew as did his preaching ministry.

One day, late in the winter, Paul Cobb brought in a new prisoner. James Russell had been apprehended in the shire while preaching to a crowd of more than sixty people. Russell had lived around London and had been converted there several years before. For some time now, he had been engaged in the ministry with the Dissenters. He had been visiting among them and preaching in Bedfordshire when apprehended.

After Paul left, the prisoners received Russell in the rather casual way they received other newcomers with whom they were not acquainted. "Well, stranger, why are you here?" bellowed a huge, burly fellow at him.

"Oh, I was just preaching over around Elstow. I am a minister in the Dissenters Church near London. I was apprehended and imprisoned here," Russell said matter-of-factly.

"Well, then, ye ought to get acquainted with our most famous prisoner—our writer and preacher, the Right Reverend John Bunyan," the large man laughed as he pointed to Bunyan. Bunyan offered his hand in friendly gesture and Russell came forward to accept it.

"How happy I am to meet you, Brother Bunyan. I had heard that you were in prison but did not know which jail you were in."

"And I am pleased to make you another among my friends. All the friends of Christ are also friends of each other," John said.

"You have already been an outstanding friend to me for several years now," Russell replied.

"How so? I do not recall that I ever met you," John said.

"Oh, I was converted as a result of reading your book, *Sighs from Hell or Groans of a Damned Soul.* It was soon after its publication that a friend of mine gave it to me and I read it. It gripped my heart, and I was soon brought to Christ. That, sir, is a good book."

John's face lighted up with pleasure. "Thank God that He made it an instrument of salvation to your soul."

"Not only to mine, but to many other souls, too, for I have often used passages from it to warn the impenitent in my preaching."

✝ ✝ ✝

Spring came with its promise of new life. John looked out the window one morning and saw the flowers blooming and the trees budding. The distant mountains had taken on a dark green hue. As he stood musing, the door opened and Paul White entered. Paul's face looked pallid. "Any trouble, Paul?" John asked.

"There may be some in the making, John. The King is marrying Katherine of Braganza. The wedding is set for May and all London is agog about it. The situation for the Puritans is still desperate. In London, jails and even lodging rooms are crowded with prisoners. I fear this marriage will not help our cause.

"Feeling is high in Parliament. With Charles marrying a Catholic, they fear it will be a repeat performance of what happened when his father did the same thing."

"Yes, we remember with sorrow some of the fruit of that marriage," said John.

"John, I regret to tell you, but you'll hear it soon doubtless anyway. Your good friend, Colonel Okey, has been executed."

John turned and looked at Paul in amazement. "I might have expected this. Sooner or later, vengeance is wreaked on a fellow who does what he feels is his duty in matters of state. Okey was associated with the execution of Charles I, and now he has been executed. Poor, dear man. He was a good brother in Christ." John stood quietly for a moment.

"Surely, Paul, it can't be the King's idea to persecute everyone who is not an Anglican."

"Not that, John. This is more likely Chancellor Hyde's notion than the King's. He runs the government."

✝ ✝ ✝

The royal marriage took place in May. A secret ceremony followed to secure Rome's sanction of the marriage. Many hoped the Queen would

113

get the King to declare another Act of Toleration. Just after the Christmas of 1663, he did announce a Declaration of Toleration. Sir John Kelynge and others, however, started at once to work for its revocation and lost no time in drawing up an Act of Uniformity. This demanded that all ministers and teachers take an oath to use the Book of Common Prayer. Despite the efforts of Roman Catholics and Dissenters, the act became a law. Only ministers ordained by an Anglican Bishop were allowed to preach. Baptists, Quakers, Roman Catholics, Dissenters and all Independents were subject to fines and imprisonment for preaching. They worshipped in barns, fields, houses and in woodlands, wherever they could manage to meet under cover of night.

John rejoiced and praised God that he was free to preach the Word without any interference. Since Paul White's conversion, John had complete freedom to *preach* in the prison, and visitors could come, as well. Often the jail was so crowded there was standing room only, for it was not illegal for persons to attend such meetings, only for ministers to preach at such gatherings. But since John and others were already imprisoned, they could do nothing with them under the new Act. John preached with great power and many were saved.

✠ ✠ ✠

One morning, in the spring of 1663, Bitsy came into the jail looking grave. "John, I do not know what we shall do with Mary. She has been very sick and seems to be in a low state of spirits this morning."

John's heart sank. Mary was his deepest love. That night John besought the Lord for her. After a long time of intercessory prayer he fell asleep. He dreamed he heard Mary calling him and awoke with a start. It was broad daylight. Knowing Bitsy would come as soon as she could, he arose and dressed. It was nearly ten o'clock before Bitsy came. John was sitting at his writing table when the door swung open, admitting her. "How is my Mary this morning?" he asked.

"She seemed a little better. She rested well most of the night. I heard her calling you once, I think, in a dream. As I was leaving, she said to tell you to come see her if you could," Bitsy said.

Great tears rolled down John's cheeks.

"Darling, please don't cry so. Mary will be all right. Dr. Banister will look after her and she will be all right," Bitsy consoled. She did not tell John about the high temperature Mary had carried in the evenings for several days, nor that Dr. Banister had not been too encouraging when he completed the examination.

Mary grew progressively worse. One morning, the next week, when Bitsy had been to visit John and was coming home, she met Paul White on the street. "Paul, would there be any way you could allow John to come home and see Mary for a little while? I fear she is dying, and I cannot stand for John not to see her before she goes. Please, if you can do anything, do help us."

"If at all possible, I surely will," said Paul as he started toward the jail.

"Paul, please don't tell John how serious Mary's illness is. It would only worry him more. He loves her so very much," Bitsy said.

When Paul reached the jail, John was sitting at his table with his head in his hands. "John, I just saw Elizabeth and she says your Mary is quite sick. I am very sorry. I'll see what I can do about allowing you to go see her tonight if we can arrange it."

About nine o'clock that night Paul came into the common room where John was seated at his writing table. "It is all right John, I made it right with Cobb. He said you could go, only to see that you were back before daybreak. We can't take any risks with the authorities."

When John knocked on the door, Bitsy came; and, seeing John standing there, she made a little cry of joy and flung the door open. He caught her up in his arms and kissed her. "Where is Mary? They let me out for the night, so I could be with her."

Bitsy took him into the family room, where they had moved Mary's bed because she was too sick to come downstairs for anything. Mary had heard her father's voice and called in a low, weak voice, "Papa, Papa, come to me quickly." Her feeble arms went about his neck and he felt the hot fever of her brow when he bent to receive her kiss. "I am so glad you have come, Papa dear. How long can you stay with me, all night?"

"Yes, dearest one, all night. I must go back just before dawn."

"Then I will stay awake and talk with you, for you are here so little, and I love you so much," Mary said, pulling him down to her again.

"No, darling, you must sleep some. I'll stay here by your bed all night, so Mama Bitsy can get some sleep."

"But Papa dear, I can sleep tomorrow, just as you can, and we can talk tonight. I may not be here to talk to you much longer. I'm getting weaker, I feel. Every day I have been thinking much about Mama and how wonderful it will be to see her. And Papa, then I'll see—I won't have to feel my way in heaven, you know," Mary said.

"But my sweet child, you must not think of going away and leaving Papa and us all." John strove hard to keep back the tears but without success.

"And Papa, there will be no jail there and no prisoners. All will be free to serve the Lord forever. No bad men like Judge Kelynge and Judge Twisden will be there. In the story of Christian, Mr. Hate-Good did not get to go to the Celestial City, did he Papa? Tell me more about Christian and his journey. I thought yesterday I got a glimpse of the Delectable Mountains out the window there," Mary said.

John's eyes filled again with tears. After a moment he said, "Mary, dear, if you insist on going to the Celestial City, then maybe I better not try to tell you more about it now. I fear I cannot tell you as well as it will be." He held her tight in his arms for a long, long time. When she dropped into a peaceful slumber, he eased her back onto the bed and sat beside her, looking at her burning cheeks in the soft candlelight. Somehow John knew now deep within his heart that Mary would not be long for this world.

While Mary slept, John and Bitsy talked much about her and the plans for her funeral, in case she did not survive. Mary tossed on her bed and cried, "Papa, Papa!"

Just before dawn Mary awoke, as if she had known her father must go. "Are you still there, Papa? What time is it? Must you go soon?"

"Yes, darling, I must go soon so I'll be back before daylight dawns."

"Thank you so much for coming, Papa. I love you so much." Mary reached for his hand and pulled him down to her face. She kissed him tenderly and hugged him with her hot arms. "You may not see me again, Papa, till you come to the Celestial City, but I'll be waiting for you. And then we can be together always, can't we, Papa?"

"Yes, always," John said, brokenly.

"Good-bye, Papa," Mary said and tried to wave at him but her hand fell limp on the bed. John slipped out the door, after Bitsy had held him in embrace, weeping and kissing him good-bye.

As John hurried along the dark streets toward the jail, he felt an urge to break and run. It would certainly be justified. Then he could hide in the woods during the day and slip back to Mary's bedside at night. Surely, it would not be so wicked to do this, when his child lay dying. Just then a rooster crowed. Day was almost beginning to break. John thought of Peter, who had denied his Lord and been rebuked by the crowing rooster. Then there came into his mind these words of St. Paul, "Obey them that have the rule over you." He hastened his steps and reached the jail a few minutes later. Slipping the key into the lock, he let himself in and closed the door. Locking it again, he walked slowly to his writing table and sat down.

He did not know how long he had been there, when Paul White opened the door and walked in. John slipped him the key from his pocket and said, "Thank you, Paul. Only God can know what this has meant to me. I think my sweet Mary will soon be in glory."

✝ ✝ ✝

The next morning about five o'clock, Mary aroused from a deathly stupor in which she had lain all night. "Papa, Mama Bitsy, I'm going now," she said.

"Papa is not here, dearest. He cannot come," Bitsy explained.

"I know. Tell him I'll see him in the Celestial City...." her words trailed off. A few moments later she aroused from the stupor and said, "Mama Bitsy, do you see Mama, my Mama? ... She's standing at the foot of my bed. Ah, how beautiful she is...."

Bitsy did not answer. Mary fell back into a stupor and was soon unconscious. Her breathing became labored and in about half an hour she drew her last breath. Bitsy folded her frail hands across her chest and went to the neighbors' house to tell them of her passing. The sun was rising in the morning sky as Bitsy returned with the neighbor lady to her home.

When Bitsy came into the jail a little later, John read the message she brought in her face. Throwing her arms about him, she sobbed out the words, "She's gone, John."

When Bitsy could control herself, she told John Mary's last words to him. John sat quietly for several moments, Bitsy sitting on his lap with her head on his shoulder. "Christian ... Pilgrim ... the Celestial City ... the Delectable Mountains...." John mumbled to himself between his sobs. "Mary enjoyed that story as no other child ever did, I do believe...., Sometime maybe I'll write the story ... in memory of my sweet Mary...."

"Yes, darling, it would be so grand if you could."

"You must go now, Bitsy. It will be hard on the children alone there with only the neighbors. Are they preparing Mary for the funeral? I'll contact Paul this morning and see what I can do to help with the arrangements," John said, as they arose from the chair.

✝ ✝ ✝

Two days later, the vicar of St. Cuthbert's preached Mary's funeral. Paul Cobb accompanied John to the church, allowing him to sit with Bitsy and the family. After the service, Mary's body was placed beside her mother's under the huge spreading tree near the Ouse River, in the old church burying ground.

Bitsy and the children accompanied John Bunyan and Paul Cobb back to the jail and spent an hour or so with him before time to return home. John explained carefully to little Elizabeth and Thomas and John that Mary had gone to be with Jesus and their mother in the Celestial City. Then he told them again about Christian and his journey to that city. "I had not told you yet all about Christian's entrance into the city, but Mary has arrived there ahead of him. She has entered into the Holy City and is now with Mama and the angels."

"Can Mary see now, Papa?" John asked.

"Yes, thank God, our Mary can see now! She has her sight forever."

"Then she is better off than if she had stayed here and never could see, isn't she, Papa?" Thomas asked.

"Yes, yes, far better off. We shall miss her much, but we must never regret that she has gone to the Celestial City. We shall all go there, too, some day."

✠ ✠ ✠

That night, John sat gazing out the window at the stars. "My sweet Mary; somewhere out there, I know you are with Christ. No more blindness, loneliness, cold or hunger, and good things shall always be yours. No more need I fear what shall happen to you, my darling one, and no more need I worry about my going first and leaving you to the sorrow of the world. I must remain here and work. I must write even more books. Yes, Mary dear, in memory of you, someday I'll write the story of Christian and the journey to the Celestial City but not now, it is far from finished."

John was hardly aware that he had been talking to himself. A cool breeze blew through the window. John looked at the clock. It was now almost ten. He was restless and could not sleep, so he moved the candle over to the holder just over his table and sat down and began to write. When the town crier cried, "One o'clock, and all's well," John lifted his hand from the sheet of paper he had been working on. At the top stood the number ten. He had written the brief outlines for a future book, *The Resurrection from The Dead.* Mary's passing had served to inspire a new book which would someday bless thousands. He placed the manuscript into the table drawer to give to Bitsy later for safe keeping at the house.

✠ ✠ ✠

As the summer months approached, John was restless. Preaching crowds had dropped off. People were busy in their fields all week and sometimes neglected the house of God on Sundays. John spent much time in writing. During that summer he wrote the draft for a new book called *Christian Behaviour*. In it he outlined the duties of Christian husbands and wives, children to parents and servants to masters. He stated clearly the disciplines of the Christian life. In this book he was at his best in similes and symbolisms, illustrating the Christian life. As he finished reworking and correcting it, Bitsy took it home and faithfully copied and prepared it for the publisher. By fall, the book was in London and getting into print. Thousands were blessed by its message. Thus the fame of Bedford's tinker-preacher spread even farther. As winter approached, he worked on another book called *Serious Meditations*. It came out just before Christmas and added further to Bunyan's fame.

✝ ✝ ✝

Christmas without Mary was sad. John did not go home that Christmas, but the family spent a portion of the day with him in the jail, bringing the customary dinner and sharing with him gifts and presents. John told the children he had been too busy to work much on the story of Christian, and he told them instead about St. George and the dragon.

Early in January, John was working on another book. It seemed that Mary's death left a vacuum in his life. He needed more spiritual activity. It drove him on in his work as nothing had done for a long time. This book he titled *Ebal and Gerizim, or The Blessing and Curse*, taking his cue from the Old Testament story of how the children of Israel stood on the mountains of Ebal and Gerizim and shouted the blessings and cursings of the Law back and forth across the valley between. This book had a good sale, too. From these three books, the Bunyans had more for their material needs than they had had for some time.

Early one morning, Bitsy came to the jail. "I have news for you, John, dear, news that will make your ears tingle and your heart beat faster," she said teasingly.

"What news could be as good as that, dearest one?"

"It's a letter from your publisher. He says people are calling for another Bunyan book. Do you have anything on the anvil?"

"Well, there's that manuscript for which you have the outline. We could work it up in a few weeks. Suppose you bring it over this afternoon and let me start on it."

"I'll be right over with it as soon as I get your dinner," Bitsy said. "Got anything else in mind?"

"Yes, I have kept something hidden under my bed," John explained, looking a bit sheepish.

"You've kept something hidden from me?" Bitsy scolded teasingly. "Bring it out right now, or I shall cut down your meals," she said.

John brought out a manuscript of many pages which he had worked on and rewritten until it was almost a perfect copy. Bitsy took it and looked at the top for the title but there was only a blank space. "What's the name of this one going to be? Are you starting a new game—writing books without titles?" she laughed softly.

"I cannot decide, it seems. I know what I want to call it, but I fear it may not be a good title."

"All right, out with it and we'll see what we think of it."

"I want to call it *Prison Meditations*. If St. Paul could write some of his best books and reflections in prison, I just wondered if I couldn't do something like this, too."

"I think it would be a wonderful title. It's different, and since you are in prison, why not make the most of it? I believe this will actually help sell the book," Bitsy encouraged. She started turning through the book. "Why, John, dear, you have completed this book already! Didn't you want me to help you with it as I've been doing? Are you trying to get rid of your secretary-wife?" she laughed.

"Oh, never, never; it was just that, since I couldn't seem to get a title for this one, I decided to keep working on it till I got it done and ready for the printer."

John then inscribed the title onto the manuscript, and Bitsy took it with her. The next day she sent it to London by Mr. Harrington, who was going there on business and would see that John's publisher received it.

That afternoon Bitsy returned with the manuscript outline for *The Resurrection From The Dead*. "I shall never forget when I brought this home. It seemed Mary was present in almost every scene described even in the notes," she said as she handed John the bundle of papers.

"Yes, I was in the *resurrection mood* then, in an extraordinary way. I just hope I can recapture a lot of that as I try to finish up the book," John murmured.

When Bitsy rose to go home sometime later, the sun's shadows were growing long on the wall of the shop across the street from the jail. As she lifted the jug in which she had brought John his dinner soup, he remarked, "Mary used to love to bring that jug to me with soup or milk in it. I used to keep the large brown papers you used for stoppers. You know, it was on these brown papers that I sketched out the outlines for the story of Christian and his journey to the Celestial City. They are folded neatly and hidden away. I guess I had better let you take them home someday."

"Really, John, is that what you wrote that story on?" Bitsy's eyes grew large.

"Yes, that is right. It's in my mind now so firmly I'll possibly not ever need the outlines, but I'll give them to you sometime, just the same." John was silent for a time. "Bitsy, one thing about that jug. I want us to keep it forever, in memory of Mary. She liked it so much, and used to bring it so often to me."

"Yes, darling, by all means. I'll not even bring soup or milk in it any more—we'll put it up in your library, where it will not get broken," Bitsy said as she slipped out of the door.

John went to his writing table and sat down and began again to write. For some time now he had been writing a book he thought might be called *The Holy City*. He, Russell, and the Quaker, Green, often discussed various problems which related to the work, and then John would write some more.

One day in the fall of 1664, as John sat writing at his table, Bitsy came into the jail. She looked troubled. When she came to his chair she said, "John dearest, I'm sorry to tell you this but I've had to sell your anvil—the one you worked so hard to buy when you moved here from Elstow. I could do nothing else it seemed. The children needed some clothes and I knew we had no money. The braiser here in Bedford saw it and wanted it, so I thought best to let him have it."

John dropped his head. It troubled him deeply but he could not hurt Bitsy—she had done with it the best she could and after all, would he ever need it again? "Sold the anvil, Bitsy? Of course it's all right, dear girl. Whatever you do in trying to keep the children together is all right."

After Bitsy was gone, he sat trying to write, but the thought of his precious anvil being gone troubled him. It was this anvil he had been carrying and dropped on his toe when he swore so loudly as to draw the burning rebuke from the immoral woman at the bookshop. It had been the beginning of the end for his swearing, he remembered. He recalled many interesting experiences connected with that old anvil and was sorry to have lost it.

☩ ☩ ☩

121

One day, Paul White came into the jail looking worried. "What news do you bring?" John asked.

"The black plague has struck again, this time in Holland. The London City Council has met to figure out how it may be kept out of London."

"I only hope we do not have another plague of this kind. It took my mother away. Are there many cases?"

"I know not how many cases there be, but enough that many are scared in London," Paul said.

John thought for a long time when Paul left. Later he and Russell and Green discussed the matter. They decided to offer their services to help if it struck in the area, and they were needed.

No more news of the plague came for some time. Then one day Cobb came into the jail and said to John, "Two Frenchmen died recently in Drury Lane. We can only hope the plague does not strike here."

During the late fall and early winter the threat died down and people hoped it had passed. But early in the spring it broke out in the parishes of St. Andrews, St. Holburns, and elsewhere. By mid-April, five people a week were dying of it. May's cooler weather again checked it, but with the coming of June, it spread again and began to grow to epidemic proportions.

One morning, Bitsy came into the jail. As soon as Paul let her in she came to John's writing table. Her face was white and drawn. "Oh, John, I fear Thomas has the plague. He is so sick and is vomiting and crying with pain," she said, sobbing.

"Oh, no, I hope not, surely," John said, his heart sinking with a certain deep-seated fear. "Did you get Dr. Banister to see him?"

"No, darling, I have no money to pay him," she sobbed.

Paul, who had overheard the conversation, said, "I'll send a lad for him, John, and I'll pay the doctor's bill, never worry." He dashed out of the jail door and was gone.

Shortly after Bitsy got home, Dr. Banister came and examined Thomas thoroughly. "I think it is nothing more than a good old-fashioned grippe.† He should be over it in about a week. Give him plenty of hot tea and soup and milk," he said.

When he had gone, Bitsy knelt by the bed and thanked God for the good news. The next day she told John, and he rejoiced that their home had been spared the dreadful plague so far.

✜ ✜ ✜

---

† *Grippe* is an archaic term for influenza.

People were leaving London in droves all summer, just as fast as they could secure medical certificates saying they were free of the plague. The authorities were not too harsh in restricting them, for London was badly over-populated anyway.

By fall, the plague had spread into the surrounding villages near Bedford. Fear gripped the people of Bedford when in December of 1664 the plague broke out in Newport Pagnell, only twelve miles away. John sat by the fireside late into the evening musing upon the situation. He recalled that in May of that year a new and cruel law had been passed, called the Five-Mile Act. It provided that no one could convene a meeting or conventicle within five miles of any town or village for preaching or teaching. "When will this cruelty be slackened, or these vicious laws repealed," he mumbled to himself. He recalled, too, that Sir John Kelynge, who had sentenced him, had now become the Chief Justice of the King's Bench. That had sealed all hope for him, for even if he had sought a writ of error in his trial, most certainly the wicked judge who had sentenced him would not now reverse his own sentence. He doubted he would even pardon him, however humbly he pleaded, without exacting a promise that he would preach no more—which by conscience he could not make. Nor would the King pardon him, for fear of Chancellor Hyde's reactions if he did, John thought.

✠  ✠  ✠

One night, sometime later, the door opened and Paul Cobb came in. He always came late at night when he had anything special to share with a prisoner. John sat alone by the fireside, the rest of the prisoners having retired. "Just hoped I'd catch ye alone, John. Wanted to talk with ye a little about a matter that concerns ye," Paul said as he pulled up a chair. Cobb seldom ever came into the jail, unless on important business. John sat quietly, wondering why he had come tonight. Paul, a sourish man, with iron-gray hair and stooped shoulders, was aging quickly. His eyes were gray and clear, and his mouth a bit puckered and turned down at the corners.

"John, I've been thinking about ye of late. I think there's hope that ye can be gotten out of this jail soon, if ye will take my advice."

"And what advice do you offer?"

"That ye do one of two things: since ye are a good preacher and writer, if ye will apply to the Anglican Church, they might grant ye a sub-deacon's license and ye could preach for the Anglicans; or, if ye would leave off preaching altogether and simply work at your business

123

and write your books. This way ye could get your message out and still be out of jail." Paul's eyes glistened with the thought of his own wisdom.

"Paul, ye know well I could never do either of these two things. I cannot become an Anglican minister, for they would never accept me and my views; and I will never promise not to preach. God has called me and I cannot go back upon Him, ever."

When Paul saw the resoluteness of John, he became very angry. "All right, fool, rot in this old jail if this is what ye want. I come and offer freedom and ye reject it like a dunce does a pardon!"

✠  ✠  ✠

Christmas Eve, John sat by the fireside musing as he had done so often that fall. He had worked on his new book a share of the day, outlining and drafting several major sections of it. *The Holy City* was to be a treatise on Revelation. It portrayed the Church of God growing to full stature and covering the earth, not as a *political* power, but as a *spiritual* force in men's lives.

While John sat musing, the door swung open quietly and in walked Paul White. "Happy Christmas Eve, John," Paul said in a low tone, so as not to disturb anybody.

"And a Happy Christmas Eve to you, too, good sir," John returned.

"How would ye like to spend the rest of the night at home?"

"Nothing could please me so well, Paul, but I fear this will get you into trouble."

"Not tonight. Cobb says to let you go, just so you are back by daybreak. Everyone is scared to death of the plague and few will venture out."

When John reached the house the children were playing by the fireside. Bitsy let him in and he spun her around and around in his arms as he had done before when he was home for Christmas. The children shouted cheerily to him as he came into the family room, running to hug and kiss him. Elizabeth rushed into his arms. He held her tightly, thinking of his sweet Mary who had gone to be with Christ since his last Christmas at home. He lifted Elizabeth's curls up and looked at them. Just like Mary's, his sweet departed wife, their mother, he thought. She was tall and lanky. John could not believe it. Elizabeth was now thirteen years old. How fast time had flown away from him. His children were growing up without a father. Thomas and John were now good-sized boys and able to help their mother a lot.

It was late in the night when the children climbed the stairs to their room. John and Bitsy lay down on the pallet by the fireplace for the rest of the night. He held her in his arms for a long time and they talked of plans for the future. His latest book, *The Resurrection From The Dead*, had just been published and the other one Bitsy had sent to London to the printer, *Prison Meditations*, was to be released early in the coming year. The publishers had promised a good royalty on these books, and John was hopeful that their estate would improve with the coming year.

Bitsy laid in John's arms the rest of the night after she fell asleep. Poor thing, John thought, she has worked so hard and meant so much to me. What if I had not married her? What would have become of my dear children? And how lonely life would have been for me. Who would have helped me with all my manuscripts as she has done? He kissed her lips lightly, and gently pulled her closer to him. The next thing he knew, he heard the town crier announcing five o'clock. He slid off the pallet and into his clothes as quietly as possible and slipped out the door, leaving Bitsy asleep.

He almost ran part of the way back; for some unaccountable reason he felt that he must get back to the jail. He turned the key in the lock carefully and slipped into the jail and into his bed. A few minutes later Paul White entered the room. He flashed a candle into John's room, and John turned his face toward him. "It's all right, John, just a routine checkup." John said nothing. He noticed a dark figure accompanying Paul into the various rooms throughout the jail. Finally, the rounds completed, John heard a low mutter at the door, and the man was gone. Paul came to John's bedroom. "Are you awake, John."

"Yes, Paul, what's the trouble?"

"Thank God, ye came back when ye did! That was a deputy from the chief of prison inspectors. They are making a routine check this year to see if jailers are allowing prisoners special privileges. Thank God, John, ye got back in time!"

Early that morning Paul Cobb came into the common room where John sat at his writing table composing a Christmas poem for his children.

"After this, John, ye can go anywhere ye want to. Ye know when to come back better than I can tell you," Paul said, his eyes shining with delight.

"Do you really mean this, Paul?" John asked in disbelief.

"Well, I mean as long as ye have either my permission or White's, and the rest of the prisoners don't know about it," Paul corrected himself.

"Thank you, Paul. I assure you I shall never abuse this privilege. I'll always be back in plenty of time."

# chapter 14

L ate in January 1665, John was notified there would be a large gathering of believers at the jail for the coming Sunday service. He was
asked by the jail brethren to preach to them this Sunday. As he searched
his soul and the Word for a suitable text, his mind was led to St. Paul's
words, "This is a faithful saying, and worthy of all acceptation, that
Christ Jesus came into the world to save sinners, of whom I am chief"
(I Timothy 1:15). He prayed much during the week.

Sunday dawned bright and clear. A larger group than had been
expected gathered at the jail. The morning air was filled with expectancy.
A good number of people stood outside the jail who could not get into
the building. Paul Cobb opened the huge jail door, so that John could
stand in the doorway and preach both to those on the inside and those
on the outside. John stepped into the doorway, opened his Bible and
read the text of St. Paul's words. Then he said, "Today, dear friends, I am
going to preach to you upon the subject, 'Grace Abounding to the Chief
of Sinners.'"

Paul Cobb dropped his head thoughtfully. Bunyan's words had hit
their mark. John was a man of God, Paul thought to himself. He is
unafraid, no matter who he may insult, when it comes to preaching the
gospel. "Only this morning I gave him special privileges, and now he does
not hesitate to pierce me to the heart, even before this whole group."

Paul sat thinking. "I can fix him; I'll withdraw all his privileges, even
take away his pen and ink. That will throttle him down. And I can cut
out the jail services altogether, and throttle him down a bit more. That
will show him who he is to insult as he has me here today."

Paul lifted his head, a haughty feeling sweeping all over him.

Despite himself, he listened as John Bunyan gave his own testimony.
"I was once the chief of sinners, too, roaming these hills and fields,
swearing and drinking and lying and stealing. I was a no-good rascal,
condemned to die forever."

Paul Cobb was stricken by a mighty sense of his own sin. He bowed his head. Tears came to his eyes. He walked to the back of the crowd while John continued to preach. When John finished his sermon and gave an invitation, Paul Cobb came to the front and stood near John. When the hymn ended, Paul spoke up, "John, may I say a word? I stand today a convicted sinner. John Bunyan's life has shown me as nothing else ever has that his religion is true and able to do for him what religion ought to

do for a man. All my life I've been a member of the Anglican Church and supposed I was a Christian. Today, I stand a condemned, unworthy sinner, and I want prayers for my salvation." Tears were now streaming down his face, and those of many others. John called on the Quaker, Nathaniel Green, to pray. After several moments of earnest prayers, during which there were many sobs and sighs in the audience, John closed the meeting with a brief season of prayer.

Paul Cobb was first to speak up. "I believe God for Christ's sake has forgiven and redeemed my soul this day. I have never known such joy as I have today. I know now what John means when he talks about 'grace abounding to the chief of sinners.' I feel this sermon was just for my soul." Several others witnessed to having been saved that day.

After the meeting was over and the crowd was gone, Russell and Nathaniel came to John. "That was the greatest sermon I ever heard," said Russell.

"Yes it was," chimed in Nathaniel.

"John, why don't you put that sermon into a book? That would be a powerful instrument of God to convict and save sinners," Russell said.

"I had thought about starting something like that last week. I decided to try it out first and see the results," John said thoughtfully. "I believe God will be pleased to bless and use this book."

"Why not expand it and work into it some of your own experiences?" Nathaniel suggested.

John spent several weeks daily working on his new book, *Grace Abounding to The Chief of Sinners*. By spring, he had a rough draft, and Bitsy had done several chapters of it. Early in June the last draft was completed, and Bitsy copied it and sent it to the printer in London.

✝ ✝ ✝

As summer dawned, the plague came back again with a dreadful fury in London and surrounding communities. Some thought the filth of many homes and the huge rats that passed from house to house had something to do with its spread. The open sewer ditches, too, did not help.

When the plague reached its height of fury and dozens were dying daily, the authorities sent word to the prison keepers surrounding London to free prisoners as trustees, all except the worst criminals. The debtor and religious prisoners especially were favored in this action. It was requested that where possible such prisoners help in the plague-stricken areas.

Paul White came into the jail to give John the news. "John, we have orders to release the debtor and religious prisoners on their behavior while the plague is raging, but the officials are also requesting that you give whatever help you can to the stricken areas."

"That I will gladly do. I have been wondering what could be done to help these dear people. Possibly a little religious assistance will also be appreciated right now," John said firmly.

"No doubt it is needed. Do what you can. You need not report back here," White said, "till there is a general call for all prisoners to return to their prisons. Maybe this plague has softened up old Hyde's heart a wee bit." Paul laughed as he started to leave.

John gathered up his clothes and other belongings eagerly. He almost forgot to go by his writing table and take out all the manuscripts he had left there. In a few minutes he was on his way home.

Bitsy's face lighted with joy when she saw her husband. "Well, at least you can breathe the air of freedom for a little while. Maybe the government will change its policy now."

"Don't be too hopeful of that," said John. "But at least we'll take the respite with all the joy we can. God knows there's a need for help in the plague-stricken communities. Paul White said nurses are very scarce in London. Male nurses are needed. Door after door has the dreadful cross on it, warning people to stay out. The death rate is very high. Often one hears the call in the street, 'Bring out your dead!' as the death wagon rolls along."

"But John, what if you get the plague? It would be so awful if you died there alone, without even me to minister to you."

"Bitsy, dearest, when we do God's service we are safe as long as we are in His hands. The doctors say it's the pus from the boils that can so easily infect others. They recommend that one who waits on these patients use great caution not to get infected in sores on the hands or about the body. One must wash his hands in strong soap often, too, when caring for them. I will take every precaution," John promised.

✜ ✜ ✜

Three days later John was astride a horse heading for London. In his saddlebags were his Bible, a hymn book, several changes of clothing and his pen and a little paper for writing.

On the second morning, he arrived at the home of an outstanding Dissenter pastor in the city. He had decided to go to his parish for his work. Pastor Jones received him with great joy. "Oh, my brother, you could not have come at a better time. There is much work to do, and many sinners are turning to God under the fear of the plague. The plague has brought so many deaths that the government has lifted the ban on services in the non-Anglican Churches. Ministers can now have the funerals for their people and conduct services of comfort for the bereaved, where they could not before. We have had large crowds in attendance at the Sunday services."

As John went about the parish ministering to the sick and dying, his fame soon spread abroad. Many sought the Lord in the homes where he ministered. The dying cried for mercy, and John pointed them to the "Lamb of God that taketh away the sin of the world."

One day, a customer approached a businessman in a store. "Is it true that the famous John Bunyan, the writer and religious prisoner, is in London, waiting on cases where the plague is raging, as I have heard?"

"You have heard correctly, sir. I just saw him the other day. He's a fine man, I tell you. You should meet him sometime," the businessman replied.

"I've read several of his books and should like to hear him preach sometime," the man said. And so from person to person, Bunyan's fame spread almost like a legend.

One Sunday, Bunyan was asked to preach at Cambridge, the seat of the university. Dr. Smith, a brilliant professor there, had heard of Bunyan and had generally been opposed to him as a ranter and disturber of the peace. After Bunyan's powerful sermon that day, Smith approached him. "How do you have authority to preach as you do when you are but an unlearned tinker?"

"Sir, I have the authority of God's Word: 'As every man hath received the gift, so let him minister it' is St. Peter's own word. Is that sufficient for you?"

"Can you read the Scriptures in the original languages?" Smith shot back at him.

"No, I cannot," Bunyan replied. "Do you have the originals?" Bunyan asked him.

"No, but I have a good copy," Smith replied.

"And I believe the English Bible to be a true copy, too," Bunyan retorted. The crowd standing around roared in laughter.

"You can't reason with an uneducated dunce," Smith snapped as he turned away.

"Nor sometimes with an educated fool," Bunyan shot back at him. Laughter ran high as the two men separated.

As the summer went by the plague lessened. Bunyan was called upon to minister in many places. He preached in Town Hall to over 2,000 people on one Sunday. Great conviction swept over the meeting and several hundred were moved to tears. Many filed down the aisles toward the improvised inquiry rooms when the sermon was finished.

A clerk reported to the Lord Mayor of London on Monday morning about the meeting. The Lord Mayor had never met Bunyan but was anxious to know about him. "I think he is the most descriptive and powerful preacher I ever heard. He has the utmost command of our language. His symbols and illustrations are very powerful and convincing," the clerk told the Mayor.

✝ ✝ ✝

By September, John was ready to return from his London mission. The Dissenters Church in London had a great farewell for him at which he preached a challenging message of the gospel. His ride to Bedford was uneventful, giving him much time to reflect upon the work done in London, the many new friends made and the plans for future work. His visit to his publisher had been most fruitful, with a promise to raise the royalties.

When he came home Bitsy welcomed him with open arms. He spun her around and around as was his custom upon arriving home, and held her tight in his arms for a long time. The children all clamored for their turns at hugging and kissing him and showering him with affection. Elizabeth clung to her father and wept for joy that he was home. "Oh, Papa, do you have to go and leave us again like this? It's almost worse than your being in prison, for us," she murmured.

"Maybe not, dearest one; we'll see, for we never know one day what another holds in this life," John said.

"Darling," said Bitsy, "I've loved your letters and read them over and over, but I've been like a flower in the sun without water or shade, almost withering away, in your absence. And I have finished recopying all the manuscript you left with me on *Grace Abounding to The Chief of Sinners*. It is rich and beautiful. You really wrote an autobiography here, in the way you used your experiences to illustrate your message. Dear, did you intend to do this, or was it just the way you illustrated the truths you wrote about?"

"I guess it was both," concluded John. "I think possibly if you may call it an autobiography, it was more or less unconsciously done; that is, I did not start out to write such a story, but as the writing unfolded, I saw that my own experiences made good illustrations of the things I wanted to make plain. I guess this is more or less how it happened."

"It surely was interesting to recopy," mused Bitsy. "There were not too many corrections to be made, either. You wrote with a passion and a tenderness that is amazing. There were many things in it which I did not know about you before. But as I read these and recopied them, it just made me love you all the more."

"Well, Betsy, dear, the publisher is giving me a raise in royalty for this one. The books have sold so well that he is sure he can do this on my next book. I brought home a good check from the last ones. *Christian Behaviour*, and *Serious Meditations* have sold extra well. *Ebal and Gerizim* did not go too well, but the others far more than counter-balanced this one, and he did not really lose anything on it. Did you get *The Holy City* manuscript finished, too, while I've been away?"

"Yes, dear, I finished that first. It's all ready for the printer. I would have sent it, but I did not know your wishes on the matter."

"Well, let's get it into the mail."

John saw Cobb that afternoon in his office in Bedford. "Well, I'm back and ready to return to prison whenever required, Paul," Bunyan said in his usual quiet way.

"I have been expecting ye almost any time now. I figured you'd know when to come in as ye always seem to, John," Paul said with a wide grin. "Tell me something of your work in London."

John related some of the highlights of his summer's work and the preaching services and conversions.

"Well, John, there's no order come down yet calling prisoners back to the jails. I expect there's quite a bit ye'd like to do about the house for awhile, so we will not bother about asking ye to return to the jail till we get some further orders. Just don't leave town without my knowledge and permission, not even to go to Elstow. We never know when some idle tale-bearer may come into town and carry the news out that ye are not in the jail."

"Thank you, Paul."

On the way home, John stopped by the home of the braiser who had purchased his anvil and asked if he would sell it back to him. The braiser said he had recently purchased another one and that John might have this one free if he wished it. He explained that he had bought it largely to help Elizabeth out when she was in such difficulty. John thanked the man, lifted the anvil to his shoulder and strode home with great joy bubbling in his heart.

That fall, John worked on his house, making many needed repairs and did considerable work in the shop. As soon as word got around that he was at home, many brought in things for him to do in order to help him.

The next two years were much the same for Bunyan. He worked in his shop by day and did a little writing at night. The children were fast growing up, and he often read to them from some of his several books by the candlelight at night, while Bitsy sat by and contentedly knitted or spun yarn for their clothes.

✝ ✝ ✝

The last day of August 1666 found John riding Mr. Harrington's horse toward London to seek an audience with the King. He had received a large check from his publisher. *Grace Abounding* and *The Holy City* had sold beyond John's fondest expectations. Thousands of copies of each had been sold and the royalty check had been most welcome.

Reaching London's outskirts, the second day of his journey, he saw high billows of smoke floating over the city. The wind was rising, and there were streams of people on horses, in carts and in wagons leaving the city. John stopped one of the riders and asked, "What does all this mean?"

"Man, haven't you heard? London is on fire and burning fast. There be little anyone can do to quench the fires. Are ye just coming to the city?"

"Yes, I have just this morning arrived from Bedford."

"Then ye better return thither or ye may lose your life. 'Tis not uncommon for this to happen. People are looting and killing," the stranger said.

"But I have started to see the King and I cannot well turn back now," John exclaimed.

John rode on toward the city, sometimes almost suffocating. At last, he reached the parsonage of Pastor Jones at the Dissenters Church.

While staying at the Jones' parsonage, John learned that the conflagration had begun in many of the small shops located on London bridge. Someone had been careless with fire. Once it had reached the thatched roofs it became uncontrollable. John went out with others to help in fighting the fire. As they were doing what they could on one of the streets, John saw a majestic coach approaching.

"The King, the King," shouted a company of people.

"Now is my chance," John thought. "I'll ask him for an audience."

As the carriage came near, John approached it. An armed guard raised his sword. "What do ye mean, you rogue? Stand back or I'll *slay* you."

John called out loudly, "Your Majesty, I must see you!"

"Find out what the fellow wants," said the King.

"What is your business?" the guard asked John.

"I bear a petition from the King's subjects in Bedfordshire," John explained.

"Have the fellow come to the palace this afternoon," the King commanded.

At the palace, John was informed that the King had left for his country estate. He decided to ride out to the King's estate and inquire for him there.

Upon arriving at the country mansion, John was told that no one was to see the King. It happened, however, that the Queen overheard John. "Bring the man to me," she commanded. "What is your concern?" she asked pleasantly. John bowed before Her Royal Majesty.

"Your Majesty, I have a petition from the people of Bedfordshire, for the King."

The Queen glanced at the writing John presented to her. As she was a Roman Catholic and her church was also under ban, she thought this would be a good way to appeal to the King. "Follow me," she said.

The King sat up on his couch as they entered his chamber. "What is this?" he said. "Who is the stranger?"

"He brings a petition to you from the people of Bedford," the Queen replied.

"Let me see it," replied the King.

"Your Gracious Majesty, We, the people of Bedfordshire do hereby most humbly petition you to make a Declaration of Freedom for all men in matters of Christian worship...."

The King read the brief petition and frowned at the names attached.

"Are you John Bunyan, the tinker who preaches and writes and who had been imprisoned in Bedford for preaching without a license?"

John felt his knees tremble, but he straightened himself and replied, "I am, Your Majesty."

"Your friends place much store by you to send you with this petition. It is not often that a prisoner brings a petition to his King!" Charles smiled faintly as he spoke.

"Your Majesty, I have been imprisoned for the sake of conscience."

"You profess to be a loyal subject, and yet disobey the laws of the land?" the King asked.

"Our Bible says we must obey God rather than man when the laws of God and man conflict," John replied quietly. "We beseech you to correct the laws of the realm, so that all men may worship God according to their conscience without breaking the law."

The King did not reply.

"The people have asked for an honorable and proper thing," the Queen put in.

King Charles looked at her. "All right, tinker," he said, "I promise to look into this matter. Now be gone and disturb me no more."

"I hope he will grant the Declaration of Freedom," John said to the Queen outside.

"Do not worry. I shall not let him rest until he does," the Queen promised.

Bunyan rode home in great peace of mind. He prayed much of the way that God would help the King to see that the petition he had left with him would be granted.

✠ ✠ ✠

John had been home only a few weeks when Paul Cobb came over one evening. "John, I regret to tell you, but the order has come demanding that all debt and religious prisoners be returned to prison."

"Well, there is always one thing I can do when I'm back in prison write!" John laughed softly.

The next morning John returned to prison.

After a few months, Paul Cobb told John he could have his freedom during the daytime, but he must report in the evenings and remain in jail overnight.

There were fewer jail preaching services now, as there were not many prisoners any more. The great plague had left its mark on the country. The Dissenters were becoming clever at disguising their meetings. They were growing in numbers, too, and officials were getting tired of enforcing the religious laws.

Despite a fair income from his books, it was nowhere near enough to keep John's family. He tagged laces all day and sold them on market days. This left him little time for writing, but he never lost his love for it. The government had begun to ban religious books produced by the Dissenter and Puritan groups. This meant that John's books had to be sold with utmost care and in far fewer numbers than before.

As the spring of 1670 dawned, John grew very impatient and restless. It had now been four years since he had petitioned the King. That spring, the countryside swarmed with constables and sheriffs, searching for religious books and any other writings. Bitsy managed to keep John's notes for *Pilgrim's Progress* well hidden.

"Has the King entirely forgotten his promise about the matter of freedom?" John wondered. Then he remembered that Charles had been busy with affairs of state. In 1667, the Dutch had sailed into the English territorial waters, captured the *Royal Charles* and burned other vessels. To keep the peace, the Dutch colony of Nieuw Amsterdam (New York) was given to the English in return for the colony of Guiana (Suriname). Longingly, John began to remember Cromwell's vigorous rule.

Moreover, John heard rumors that the King was tired of his Roman Catholic wife and wished a divorce. Charles wanted to marry Frances Stuart, a virtuous woman with whom he had become infatuated. Lord Clarendon's power was broken, and his influence for the Christian cause of freedom would be no more felt by the King. It surely was a dark and dreary Saturday night as John retired to his room.

✝ ✝ ✝

That fall, the King sent a message to the Anglican Churches to take an offering for "the poor enslaved English Christians, captured in Algiers." Bitsy reported it to John. John reached into his pockets and found a sixpence. Tossing it to Bitsy he said, "There, put this in the offering at St. Cuthbert's. Let it never be said that John Bunyan would not give to the poor enslaved Christians."

"It is an odd world, John. The King raises money for Englishmen imprisoned in Algiers, and will not free Englishmen imprisoned in this country for no greater crime than preaching without a license," Bitsy said as she placed the sixpence into her purse.

In January 1671, John received a letter from the venerable Dr. John Owens of London, saying that he had talked with the King about the Declaration and that the King had promised to look into the matter.

Months passed with nothing happening, and John became increasingly discouraged.

✝ ✝ ✝

Another spring came around. The rector of Northill, Edward Fowler, published a book titled *The Design of Christianity.* When John read this new book he was deeply moved. To him it was anything but true Christianity. In about six weeks, he wrote a reply to it, writing with fury, for he was deeply stirred. He called his reply *The Doctrine of Justification.*

Fowler, a clergyman who had been ejected during the early Restoration period, but who had made his peace with the authorities, wrote in his book that a minister should do whatever the government commanded, or custom demanded, in order to carry on his work.

John demanded of Fowler what a man should do if he were in Anatolia (Turkey). Should he accept Mohammed as Lord? "How any servant of Christ can face two ways at the same time I cannot understand!" he stormed, "I'll put Mr. Fowler in my story about Christian and call him Mr. Facing-both-ways." He laughed heartily. "I suppose this character could also portray William, Earl of Bedford, since he first fought for Cromwell, then turned for the King."

✠　✠　✠

In mid-July, a special order reached Bedford regarding prisoners held for offenses against the church. It was a sultry morning. The jail door opened early, and Paul Cobb stood in the doorway. "Call all prisoners to the common room," he said, a glad note in his voice. When the men gathered Paul announced that all religious prisoners were free. "Gentlemen, it is with great pleasure I open this door to you."

Bitsy was standing in the yard of their house, when John walked up with his belongings. She had heard nothing of the recent edict. Throwing down the hoe with which she was working the flowers, she ran to John, crying, "John, darling, are you really free?" John flung down the things he was carrying and took her into his arms, spinning her around and around, dancing for joy on the lawn.

"Yes, Paul Cobb read us the edict this morning."

They went into the house. Elizabeth, now almost a grown girl, was swept off her feet into her father's arms, "Papa is free for good; they read the edict to the prisoners this morning, freeing them," Bitsy told Elizabeth.

She screamed for joy and hugged her father as tightly as she could. "Oh, Papa, Papa, how wonderful! Now you can go with me to walk in the woods and gather wild flowers. I have wanted you to go with me, oh so many times."

# chapter 15

Weeks went by and John never lifted his pen to write a line. He was so enchanted with his freedom and the joys of working in the shop and walking in the woods and puttering around the house that writing drifted out of his mind. But he was awakened to its power in a rude manner when his friend, Dr. Owen of London, sent him a copy of Dr. Fowler's evident reply to his book on *The Doctrine of Justification.* The little book was titled, *Dirt Wiped Off,* and was a scathing attack, for what it called the "gross ignorance, erroneousness, and most unchristian and wicked spirit of John Bunyan, lay preacher in Bedford."

The next day found John at his writing desk for the first time since leaving the Bedford jail. Peeping over his shoulder, Bitsy saw the heading of his work, *Differences in Judgment About Water Baptism, No Bar to Communion.* His hand fairly flew over the pages. He wrote as a disturbed man, but yet in clear, concise terms easily understood. In this treatise he said, "The saint is a saint before water baptism, and may walk with God, and be faithful with the saints and to his own light also, though he never be baptized." John's book closed the mouth of Fowler and his friends.

John now gave most of his time to his braising business and preaching over the countryside. His popularity continued to grow. His most outstanding book to date, *Grace Abounding to The Chief of Sinners,* had made him widely known. In this book he had set forth his conversion and the early struggles he had in the Christian life in such a way as to be very helpful to many readers. It was really an autobiography of John's own spiritual struggles and early days in prison. It had a large sale and made him far more widely known than any of his other works.

One day when John was busy working, Bitsy came into the shop. John noticed that she acted a bit shy. "I don't know how to tell you, John, but plain words are the best. We are going to have a baby!"

John looked up from his work at the anvil. His face was radiant, "Well, my dearest, how could you have pleased me any more? You are a sweet wife. If it is a girl, I know now what we'll name her, Sarah." When the child put in her appearance, they named her Sarah as John wished. Bitsy was more happy and contented than she had been during their entire marriage.

Early in 1672, it was decided by the Bedford Meeting that John should be their pastor. After the deacons decided to present his name to the church, a day of prayer and fasting was called. One of the now-famous Fenne brothers and Mr. Harrington were chosen to notify Bunyan of his call. "You have been true to your Christian beliefs," the men said in their approach. "Your usefulness has grown, and you can prove an effective agent for the cause of God as the pastor of our Bedford Meeting. The flock needs a shepherd, and the Bedford Meeting needs you."

Bitsy's eyes grew wide as she listened to the report of the committee and its decision to call her husband as pastor. On the following Sunday morning, John accepted the invitation.

⊹ ⊹ ⊹

Early in the year 1673, John took into church membership an attractive young woman, Agnes Beaumont. She seemed unduly attracted to him but John paid her no attention. She was a faithful and dutiful member, though she was often kept away by an ungodly father.

One clear, cold day in February, John stopped at the home of Agnes Beaumont's brother for some warm milk. Agnes Beaumont lived with her father next door. She hurried over to the home of her brother, hoping to go with John to meeting. John was almost ready to depart when Agnes came in.

"Good morning, Brother Bunyan," Agnes smiled at him cheerfully.

"And a good morning to you, Agnes," John replied.

"Could I ride with you to the meeting today, Brother Bunyan. I have no other way to go."

Her brother spoke up, "Agnes will be very disappointed if she cannot go. Your preaching gives her great spiritual help."

Bunyan was dumbfounded. "I will not take her," he said.

"There's no reason why she shouldn't go, since you are going straight to church, is there?" the brother insisted.

"Well, I suppose then I can take her," John replied, not wishing to offend them. But he was not happy about the decision.

Agnes was dressed in a few moments and climbed on the horse behind John. They set out across the country for the meeting house. As they rode over the seven miles to the church John talked to Agnes of many things regarding her spiritual welfare.

Agnes was twenty-two years old. "Oh, how fortunate I am today to be riding behind so great a man as Mr. Bunyan. How I wish the whole of England could see me today! I am indeed a queen," Agnes said to herself. Bunyan's exhortations rebuked her.

The horse almost fell in the snow. "Oh, you almost lost me, Mr. Bunyan! I must hold tight or be thrown off! I hope you don't mind."

"Hold on only if you must to keep from falling," John advised her, wishing she would release her firm hold. In all his forty-four years he had never been any more miserable. He did not wish to discourage the young woman, but he was afraid someone might start some dreadful story about them. It was a delight and blessed relief to him to arrive at the church before anyone else.

After the meeting, John arranged for Agnes to return home with somebody else. When Agnes returned home, her father was furious and refused to allow her to enter the home, unless she promised not to go to church any more. Agnes was compelled to spend the night in the barn. The next morning, after further angry words, the father admitted her into the house. On Tuesday, he died of a convulsion.

✝ ✝ ✝

At this point, a young attorney named Farrow started to spread rumors. He had wanted to marry Agnes, but had been turned down by her and was still hurt.

"I guess you heard about Agnes Beaumont riding to church behind Pastor Bunyan," he said to a neighbor. "In my opinion Bunyan gave her poison for the old man's coffee. You wait and see. Bunyan will marry that girl."

"I don't believe a word of such nonsense," the neighbor said shortly.

The neighbor went to Solomon Beaumont with this story. Both agreed readily that an autopsy would be needed to protect the good names of both Agnes and the minister. The funeral was held up and autopsy performed, which proved the old man had died of natural causes. Nevertheless, young Farrow's story continued to spread.

Other details of gossip were added. A minister at Baldock Fair had very little use for Bunyan because of his powerful preaching against the common sins of the times and against the formality of the established churches. He claimed that Agnes and Bunyan had been guilty of immoral behavior. Another tale stated that Bunyan was a widower desirous of marrying Agnes as soon as her father was dead. Still another tale claimed that John lived with two different wives!

John Wilson decided something had to be done. He went to see his friend John Bunyan.

"I am glad you came to tell me. Thank you for being a friend as you have always proved to be, John," Bunyan said. Dropping his head for a moment of thought, he finally said, "John, you know my enemies have never let me rest; it has been so most of my life. But this time they over-shot the mark."

"This I know, John, without doubt," said Wilson. "I guess we can do nothing but let the tales run their course and die of their own accord."

"I think you are right, John."

When Wilson left, John went into the house and told Bitsy the stories that were circulating.

"John, darling, don't you know that it is the very trick of Satan? These things cannot hurt your ministry—not for long at least, if you are faith-ful to God. At least those who believe them will say that you are well qualified to preach about sin!"

✠   ✠   ✠

The Bunyans invited Agnes to their home. "Bitsy and I don't know how all these tales could have started," John said. "Since we were not seen by anyone that I recall, there is no foundation for these tales."

"Oh, I know how part of it started," Agnes explained. "After we left that day, Farrow came to urge me again to marry him. Solomon told him I had ridden behind you to church and would not be home until evening. He went back to Newport and deliberately planted the lies. And Brother Bunyan, I see now what evil my own tongue has done. I have made remarks to two or three of the sisters in the church that I loved you very much, because you had won me to Christ. I did not mean that I loved you in any bad way. God has dealt with me and I have seen the folly of my talk."

"We have all learned our lesson, and we cannot be too strong in carrying out St. Paul's admonition to 'shun the very appearance of evil,'" John said.

Soon after, John Wilson preached a powerful sermon against evil speaking in his church in Hitchin in which he defended Bunyan. People who had never before heard Bunyan now went to Gamlingay to hear him. Crowds thronged the building until there was no room for them. His fame spread far and wide. The very thing which his enemies had intended should destroy him had the opposite effect.

141

# chapter 16

One evening in January 1675, John came in from visiting and working among the people. After the evening meal, John said, "Bitsy, dearest, I bring you bad news. I learned at the market today that the King and Parliament are working on another bill to revoke the King's Declaration of Indulgence. This will mean prison again for Dissenters."

On February 3, 1675, King Charles II revoked the Declaration of Indulgence. Nonconformists were again outlawed and forbidden to preach, teach or convene conventicles of any kind. All licenses of such ministers were revoked and the magistrates and officers of the law notified to imprison all who might disobey the law.

Undaunted, John went on preaching at the Bedford Meeting just as he had been doing for years. The officers waited as long as they dared to, but finally they had no other alternative than to take John into custody. The Sheriff of Bedfordshire came to John's home and presented him with a summons for the following morning at ten o'clock. "I regret to do this, Bunyan. I shall not take you to jail tonight. This is your opportunity to cease preaching and go free, or to skip the country and escape imprisonment."

At ten o'clock the next morning, March 4, 1675, Bunyan entered the courtroom at Herne Chapel. When his case was called for and he was asked if he had broken the laws by preaching without a license, he replied, "I have broken no laws of God and have acted within my license from the King, granted to me as an ordained minister of a local congregation."

"But that license has been revoked and you are under ban from preaching at all," Judge William Foster snapped. "Do you admit your guilt before the law?" he asked.

"Your Honor, I have no guilt to confess. I have done only that which is just and right, and according to God's Word."

Judge Foster was enraged. "Bunyan shall be broken, and his stubbornness made an example for others who will not yield to their Majesty's laws of the land. Take him away to the jail to remain there until he promises to preach and teach no more, or until he rots."

John Grew, Mayor of Bedford, spoke up. "Judge, Your Honor, is there no other alternative to this prison sentence?"

"Certainly," the judge replied. "He may pay a heavy fine for all the counts against him and then the promise to cease from teaching and preaching."

Bunyan raised his hand and spoke. "Mayor Grew, there is no need for this. Neither I nor the local church here can pay this fine; and besides, were I released today, I would preach again tomorrow."

"John Bunyan is determined to break the law, come what will!" the judge roared. "Take him to prison!"

As he led the prisoner away, Paul Cobb came and said, "Well, John, I guess we will again be sharing a few of the old times we used to have at the jail."

# chapter 17

The cold winds of March had given away to April's warm breezes. John sat at his writing table, musing. He recalled what he had written a few days after he had been returned to prison. "Then I got me back into prison and did sit down to write again. I have been away from my writing too long. Maybe this is not so much a prison as an office from which I can reach the world with Christ's message."

After a Sunday service, in which John preached a sermon on the "Strait Gate" (Matthew 7:13, 14), he began writing another book—the first book in several years. He had actually begun the book toward the close of his last imprisonment but had neglected to finish it. He now saw a great light from God and was made conscious of his duty to finish this book, which he entitled *The Strait Gate*. Before the summer was ended the book was on its way to his publisher.

On February 6, 1676, Thomas Bunyan, John's father, died at Elstow. Word was brought to John in the prison. He lay there that night staring into the loft above him and wondering if his father had finally made peace with God.

✠ ✠ ✠

One day, when Bitsy came bringing him his main meal for the day, she noticed a pile of brown papers on his writing table. She thought she recognized them but was not certain. "What are these papers, John?" she asked.

"Those are the papers from the milk jug which you and Mary brought to me while I was in prison before. It is the outline of the children's story of Christian and the Celestial City. It has a sort of growing fascination for me. I think I'll create an allegory of the Christian life and the Christian's walk with God in this world."

One day, the jail door opened, and who should walk in but Russell, John's former prison mate. "Well, my good man, why are you back here?" inquired Russell.

"I was preaching in Bedfordshire and was reported to the officers."

"What is this you are working on, John?"

"It's a story I've been telling the children for several years about Christian and his journey to the Celestial City. I'd like your opinion on it."

In a few days, Russell finished reading the manuscript. "You have here one of the most masterful pieces of writing yet to come from your pen, John," Russell reported.

Several weeks went by as John continued to write on his story. Bitsy took a copy home and reworked it according to his corrections and notes, keeping nearly up with him all the time.

One day, Paul Cobb came into the prison for some reason and saw John writing. "What book are you writing now, John?"

"Well, Paul, it's a story which I have told my children over the years and now I am inclined to write out the thing for a book. It tells how Christian makes his journey through this world of trouble to the Celestial City," John explained.

"How did you ever fall upon this plan of writing?"

"I fell to musing one time and I thought of certain characters whom I had known, who had come to stand for something to me, either good or bad. I thought of a Christian man and decided to give my major character that name. Those qualities which help Christian to lead a godly life, I have personified and given names. And I have done the same with those things that hinder Christian's way."

"Do you find this easy writing, John?"

"Yes, once the form of the allegory came to me, and I began to set it down. Pure joy makes me write; it is so light a task."

✠ ✠ ✠

John worked faithfully on his story in his spare time, meanwhile preaching, teaching, and counseling whenever these ministries opened up to him. By the spring of 1677 he had his story about two-thirds done. That year the Quakers petitioned the King asking for the release from prison of certain persons whom they felt to be worthy of pardon and release, including Bunyan. The petition was signed by over four hundred.

In the meantime, the government imposed strong censorship upon all publishing. The Nonconformists had learned too well how to use the pen. The Chief Censor sent out a Censor's Band which searched for manuscripts and confiscated any they discovered. They appeared at Bedford jail in hope of finding some of Bunyan's writings. When the search was completed, the searchers looked sullenly at Bunyan as if they knew he had beaten them to their game, but left without asking any questions. They warned him to write no more in protest against the King or Parliament or, for that matter, anything of a religious nature.

The Quaker petition was successful in softening government policy toward certain imprisoned persons. Dr. Owen, John's good friend in London, went to the newly appointed Bishop of London to ask for precautionary bond for John's release from prison. Two prominent Nonconformists of London, who knew Bunyan and believed in him, signed for his surety. Late in June, when the bond reached John at Bedford, he was overwhelmed with joy to find that he had been granted release.

✛ ✛ ✛

That fall, John worked hard on completing his story of Christian. When it was completed, John insisted they invite a group in from the church to listen to the story to see if it had sufficient appeal for publication.

"Well, now! You have heard it. Is it worth publishing for young Christians?" John demanded.

Mr. Harrington, the head deacon, expressed his hearty appreciation. Mayor Grew did not agree. He felt there was too much play for attention. The young people felt Bunyan had done a superb job.

When everyone was gone, Bitsy said, "Now, John, your wife was right for once. You have a good book here. It may outsell all the others you have written."

Bunyan had taken great pains in deciding what to call his new book. Finally he said, "Well, let us name it *Pilgrim's Progress*."

The manuscript was sent to the publisher, who kept the identity of the author secret as the Censor's readers went over the work. One of the Censor's readers remarked, "You have as good a book there as any Anglican divine in England could have written, sir. I hope it has a wide circulation and brings you much money. I shall see that you have the proper license for its release by late tomorrow."

*Pilgrim's Progress* was published in 1678 and was an instant success. Within three months after it was out, a new edition was needed. It was a small book of 232 pages, but its sales soared. By 1679, the publisher, The Peacock Stationers, reported more than 100,000 copies sold.

John's days were now full of labors. There were many letters to be answered. He traveled widely over the English Midlands, preaching wherever he could. When he visited London, some of the larger meeting places were filled to capacity.

At home, John set to work on corrections for *Pilgrim's Progress* for a new edition that would soon be released. Many changes in spelling were made. The book was updated and a few additions were made. Mr. Worldly-Wise-Man was added at this time, and possibly Mr. By-ends, too.

✝ ✝ ✝

During the fleeting years that followed 1679, John wrote *The Life and Death of Mr. Badman*, hoping it would be a fitting sequel to *Pilgrim's Progress*, but the public did not accept it as such. Several other people wrote "sequels" to *Pilgrim's Progress*, but they all fell flat. Some of the writers deceitfully put Bunyan's name to their works. Such publications were short-lived and soon found to be spurious. Before 1680, he had written another allegory, *The Holy War*. Meanwhile, Bunyan's publisher insisted on a true sequel to *Pilgrim's Progress*. John showed his daughter Sarah his draft for Part II of the book. It described Christiana (Christian's wife) on her journey to the Celestial City.

John was now busy night and day, writing. It seemed the urge was upon him, as if he felt his time was short. Bitsy kept busy with the corrections and copying. Sarah, who had been well trained in school, now started helping.

One morning, Sarah came into the library. "Papa, do you realize how many books you have written in the past two years?"

"How many?" asked John.

"Well, there's *A Case of Conscience Resolved*, *The Greatness of the Soul*, *The Barren Figtree or The Doom and Downfall of the Fruitless Professor*, *A Holy Life*, and *The Beauty of Christianity*, beside the one you are working on," Sarah explained.

"Not bad, five books in two years," commented Bunyan.

"I fear you are writing too much for your own good, Papa. You need to rest more. Your preaching is heavy and this work is too draining," Sarah implored.

"My work must go on, Sarah, darling. I may not have as long to live as some. Those years in prison have left their mark. Little exercise, dark, damp, cold days without number, all took their toll. I am working against time."

"What are you working on now, Papa?"

"Oh, this is my will. Every man should leave a will you know."

The winter and spring of 1688 were spent largely at home with Bitsy and Sarah, pastoring the Bedford Meeters Meeting and writing another new book. Several times during that summer John grew short of breath and had to rest under the great willow at the back of his house. He never lost interest in his immortal dream—*Pilgrim's Progress*—and its success. It had now gone through eleven editions, the last several of which contained the sequel.

John was indeed reaping the rich harvest of his labors. Almost daily the mail brought letters of appreciation from many parts of the country, even from the New World. *Pilgrim's Progress* had reached America and was being read there with delight.

# chapter 18

One August morning Sarah brought home the mail. It contained a letter from Mark Welham, a young man in Reading, pleading for help in a domestic dispute. Although John Bunyan was not feeling well, he decided to go and give what help he could. He could never say "No" to someone in trouble.

"I can take my new book to the publisher in London," John said.

The next few days John busied himself with preparations for his trip. He notified his friends in London he would be at Whitechapel, near Petticoat Lane, for a service on the nineteenth of August. He wrote his good friend John Strudwick, who ran a grocery store in Snow Hill in London, of his intentions to be there on the seventeenth or eighteenth.

"John, dear, before you go, let us pray together," Bitsy said. Usually she left such matters up to John. Kneeling in prayer in the family room, John poured out his soul to God. Arising from prayer, John kissed them both. He held Bitsy in his arms a long time.

"Do be careful, darling," she said. "You are not as young as you once were."

By noon the next day, John reached Reading, where Mark Welham and his father lived. They had been reconciled by mid-afternoon and were rejoicing that Bunyan had come to visit them.

It was hot and muggy the next morning, but John decided to go on toward London about forty miles away. By riding hard he could reach London by nightfall.

A bad thunderstorm overtook the traveler, drenching him to the skin. As the rain continued to fall, John prayed as he spurred on towards London. "Dear God, wilt Thou not abate this rain? I am in much distress. My cold will surely be worsened by this rain."

It was night when Bunyan reached Strudwick's grocery store.

Seeing his condition, Strudwick stabled his horse and rushed him into the house and into fresh, dry clothes.

Two days later, John was up and ready to keep his appointment at Whitechapel.

The following week John did not feel too well but went about his business taking his latest manuscript to his publisher. "Oh God, bless this book as Thou hast blessed my others," John prayed. " *The Acceptable Sacrifice* is my sixtieth book. How well Thou hast helped, O Lord, to prepare these works."

During the rest of the week John visited many old friends in London. By the weekend he had come down again with a very bad cold and was forced to remain at home over Sunday. By Tuesday he was worse and Strudwick summoned the doctor. By now Bunyan was so ill the doctor advised Strudwick to notify Bunyan's family.

✠ ✠ ✠

Back home, Bitsy had been restless all Monday night. She dreamed that John had come home sick and was talking in his sleep. She heard him distinctly quoting from *Pilgrim's Progress* about Christian's going to his Father's house, and that none were to weep for him. She awoke startled, then knelt and prayed for John for some time.

On Thursday, the messenger arrived with news about John's illness. Sarah burst into tears and Bitsy's heart sank. Losing no time, they rode for London, arriving at Strudwick's on Thursday afternoon. They found John lying unconscious.

Bitsy kissed his forehead and John revived enough to recognize her. He tried to lift his hands to her face, but could not.

"Thank God you got here," he said weakly. He closed his eyes again.

John spent most of the night in delirium. Sometimes he spoke about preaching and writing. Once he opened his eyes wide and said, "Mary, my sweet Mary ... I'll soon be with you ... don't hurry off and leave me ..." Bitsy broke into tears, for she knew then that John would never leave his bed.

Bitsy and Sarah stood at the foot of John's bed. He had been unconscious for a long time. Suddenly, he opened his eyes and looked directly at Bitsy and Sarah, "Weep not for me, weep for yourselves. With great difficulty I have got hither. My sword I now give to him that shall follow me in my pilgrimage ... my scars I now carry with me to be a witness for me that I have fought His battles who now will be my rewarder." He dropped his hands on the bed and closed his eyes. He had quoted from *Pilgrim's Progress*.

Some while later, John opened his eyes and smiled when he saw Bitsy and Sarah. Then he looked upward and said, "Take me, for I come to Thee."

The immortal dreamer, the Tinker of Bedford, was dead.

Two days later, a huge crowd packed Whitechapel to hear George Cokayan preach at Bunyan's funeral. He read these simple words:

> John Bunyan, born in Elstow, England, November 30, 1628, departed this life at London, August 31, 1688, being almost sixty years of age. It is remarkably strange that this man who came into the world under such poor circumstances and lived a portion of his life under the most handicapped conditions did such a great work. Nearly twelve years he spent in Bedford Jail as a religious prisoner, suffering for the freedom he craved. He lived almost sixty years and leaves behind him exactly sixty books—a book for every year of his life. His latest book is now awaiting publication in this city and will doubtless be read by thousands as his last message to his fellowmen.
>
> The Lord Mayor of London was among Bunyan's warmest friends. As is now widely known, he was on his way homeward from the Fair on Thursday past and designed to stop and see John, but his horse threw him, and he is even now lying at the point of death. Bunyan was not only loved by the common people but was revered and respected by even the most wealthy and educated....
>
> The candle which John Bunyan has lighted in England shall never be put out. Above all his other works, *Pilgrim's Progress* already has gone far enough over many lands to see that it may become one of England's greatest contributions to the literature of this century....

Bunyan's body was laid to rest in the Bun Hill Fields Cemetery. Four days later, a memorial service was held for him in the Meeters Church, at Bedford. A day of prayer and fasting to mourn his loss was held the next day.

A group of John's admiring friends raised a subscription in London to erect a memorial to him in Bun Hill Fields Cemetery. There it stands over his grave, a carving of Pilgrim, with his staff in one hand, his open book in the other. And underneath, these simple words:

### JOHN BUNYAN

Author of the

### PILGRIM'S PROGRESS

**August 31, 1688**

**Age 60**

John Bunyan.